# DESTINATION BRANDING
## for
# SMALL CITIES

■

## The Essentials for Successful Place Branding

# DESTINATION BRANDING
## for
## SMALL CITIES

■

### The Essentials for Successful Place Branding

## Bill Baker

**Destination Branding for Small Cities**
*The essentials for successful place branding*

Published by:
Creative Leap Books
20212 SW 86th Ave.
Portland, Oregon 97062 USA

Printed in the United States of America

Designs: Gregory Thomas (*GTA Design*) and Michael Winder

ISBN: 978-0-9797076-0-5

# CONTENTS

# ACKNOWLEDGEMENTS

*Destination Branding for Small Cities* has grown from three decades of experiences at the forefront in destination marketing and branding. My journey in destination marketing started in Australia's Hunter Valley which is today one of the world's great wine tourism destinations. Over the following decade, I was also fortunate to be engaged in developing and implementing Australia's brand strategies in over 26 countries, which was possibly the finest learning opportunity any destination marketer could be given. This included launching Australia's award winning and acclaimed "*Shrimp on the Barbie*" campaign in the USA, which I managed for seven years. This was one of the pioneering efforts in branding a nation and allowed me to shape many of the ideas and techniques that are in this book.

Over the past twenty years, the journey has taken me to hundreds of locations in the USA, Australia, Canada, and many other countries, where I have been able to gain an even greater appreciation for the challenges faced by cities and regions when it comes to branding and marketing.

Over my career there have been many people who deserve my thanks for their expert advice, friendship and encouragement. I have had the privilege of working with and learning from some of the most talented destination marketing and branding experts in the world. The list of their names is far too long to mention each one. They include all of the great people from the worldwide offices of the Australian Tourist Commission (now Tourism Australia) and its outstanding advertising, public relations and research agencies, and my friends in the North American, European and Australian travel industries. My special thanks go to our clients, who have encouraged Total Destination Management to be innovative and on the leading edge by applying new concepts in our destination branding assignments.

*Destination Branding for Small Cities* has required assistance from several friends whose destination marketing expertise I greatly respect. I would like to thank Vicki Dugger (Downtown Solutions) and Eric Aebi for generously sharing their time and expertise by reviewing the manuscript and providing valuable suggestions.

I am particularly indebted to Peggy Bendel, Senior Vice President for Development Counselors International (DCI). Peggy has not only been a great friend and colleague to me over the past twenty years, but was a great inspiration throughout the production of this book. She has generously given her time and drew on her vast experience to make valuable additions.

Greg Thomas, in addition to his excellent creative work for Total Destination Management, deserves my gratitude for assisting with the cover and the diagrams that illustrate *Destination Branding for Small Cities*. I also appreciate the assistance that Mike Winder gave in the design of the cover and the final production.

My wife and business partner Joan deserves special thanks not only for her patience, but her encouragement, ideas, and constant attention to the quality of this book. Our daughters Renee and Kate are my inspiration, and I hope that this book can contribute in a small way to making a better world for them to discover and explore.

Bill Baker

# PREFACE

The prospect of developing a brand strategy for your city may at first seem like a daunting challenge. I hope this book makes the journey much easier for you. It will enable you to move the destination to new levels of performance and along the way provide many learning opportunities for you and sharpen every aspect of the city's strategic marketing programs.

This book has been written as a primer to simplify and clarify the practice of branding small cities. It is designed to demystify what can be the complex concepts and processes needed to reveal a brand that can be widely accepted by stakeholders and resonate strongly with target audiences.

This is not an academic expose, nor does it contain all of the technical elements that may be appropriate for the branding of places with substantial research budgets. We recognize the marketing efforts of most small cities rely very heavily on hard-working people who may not have a degree in marketing, who depend on part-time and volunteer staff, and who often have limited resources to engage outside professional assistance. We have tried to simplify the issues and suggest affordable, proven techniques that can be employed by destinations of all sizes.

Throughout, we use the terms "destination," "community," and "city" interchangeably to refer to the geographical entity at the heart of the brand. While the title is *Destination Branding for Small Cities* the principles and processes can just as readily be applied to regions, counties, scenic byways, Main Streets, heritage districts, suburbs, and neighborhoods. We consider a 'destination' to be a place that people will leave their present location in order to visit, shop, invest, or relocate.

We've designed the book to be particularly useful for public and non-profit organizations that must create a brand strategy through collaboration and consultation with multiple, diverse stakeholders, and within the confines of a limited budget. While the examples I have included are mainly North American, the underlying principles as well as the *7A Destination Branding Process* have universal application.

*Destination Branding for Small Cities* is a hands-on toolkit, designed to assist with brand development for communities with a population of fewer than 150,000 residents. In most cases, cities of this size can't always afford wide-ranging consumer research or high-profile advertising campaigns. Yet, there remains the need for them to stand out from the crowd in order to attract more visitors, more talented people, more inward investment, and more new businesses.

Readers of *Destination Branding for Small Cities* will find it useful as a:

- Source of practical information for branding destinations of all sizes, but particularly cities and regions
- Roadmap to guide their brand planning
- Resource to enhance brand knowledge within their organization and the community

*Destination Branding for Small Cities* outlines the essential steps for branding places where it is important for a variety of community-based organizations and stakeholders to collaborate and reach consensus. The processes, techniques and tools apply whether it is an overarching brand or for only tourism or economic development. The marketing capabilities of communities vary enormously according to their population, attractors, resources, market maturity, politics, public awareness, history, economic base, and marketing expertise.

For instance, the Las Vegas Convention and Visitors Authority (LVCVA) has a marketing budget of more than $100 million per year[1] with a worldwide reputation and a local tourism infrastructure among the most developed and sophisticated in the world. The LVCVA budget is equal to the combined budgets of thousands of smaller American cities. This certainly does not mean that these smaller locations should wave white flags and give up trying to market themselves, but it *does* mean they must have a strong strategic focus to whatever they do – and don't do.

Recommending the destination marketing practices of Las Vegas, New York City, and San Francisco to small cities is hardly appropriate. We have specifically designed this book for those ambitious communities that recognize that they must adopt the principles of a branded approach, despite having a modest budget.

Relatively small cities such as Durham NC, Grants Pass OR, and Bellingham WA, who are mentioned in this book, along with hundreds of others are doing excellent jobs in creating distinctive brands for themselves on more modest budgets.

For simplification, we refer generically to the variety of organizations responsible for the marketing and branding of their area as a destination marketing organization (DMO). This term is intended to embrace Convention & Visitors Bureaus, Chambers of Commerce, local government entities, downtown associations, Main Street associations, economic development authorities and other similar organizations that may be responsible for destination marketing and management.

Throughout, we've provided interesting examples to illustrate specific brand issues and applications. Some of these places excel in one or more aspects of their destination branding, but our reference is not meant to infer that every aspect of their programs are necessarily an excellent example of brand development. We also refer to some destinations that are not small cities. The reason for this is to demonstrate practices that are appropriate to places of all sizes.

# INTRODUCTION

There are very close emotional ties between people and the places they live. This brings an added dimension to consider when it comes to introducing practices such as branding and marketing to a community. This is a reality that the marketers of consumer goods rarely face. Whether as residents or visitors, we have very special bonds to places.

First and foremost, every community is a place where residents may have lived all of their lives, where they went to school, married, had children, and built their careers. They have deep meaning and invoke strong passions because they are also a personal reflection of them, their social status, and their life choices. Their parents and grandparents may have also shared those same passions about the place. Importantly, it may be where many of them want to spend their future, and they may want to passionately protect its quality of life and community values for future generations. These relationships can have a profound influence on the branding and marketing of a place.

Communities must constantly adjust to changing circumstances, all the while maintaining a balance with the values and vision of their residents. Those ambitious places wanting to increase their well-being and reputation through tourism and economic development need to first answer some basic questions:

- What do we want to be known for?

- How can we stand out from the crowd?

- What thoughts and feelings do we want to come to mind when people are exposed to our city's name?

These questions are at the heart of branding. To successfully answer them the community needs to be customer-focused, strategic, open-minded, and imaginative in order to reveal the brand in a way that will generate positive feelings, respect, and loyalty. It must be crystal clear about what it is, what it does, why it is interesting, and why it should matter to specific audiences.

Destinations are not homogenous. Branding these complex entities takes much more than a cookie cutter approach or an afternoon brainstorming session. What may work in revealing and building the brand for one community, may not necessarily work in another. The processes that I have outlined provide tools that can be adapted to a variety of circumstances.

Brands are very much like people, and this becomes a valuable metaphor for studying how we can apply branding concepts. A destination without a clear and appealing identity is like a person with a dull personality. They blend into the crowd, are seen as uninteresting, and don't get the attention and respect that they need or deserve. On the other hand, like a person it can have a distinctive personality, strong values and strengths, and a particular look and style associated with it.

While branding has been applied to consumer products for decades, the concept of destinations formulating brand strategies only began to appear during the 1990s. A strategic approach to destination branding was first introduced at a national level. The nations of Australia, Hong Kong, and Spain were among the first to truly embrace the practice. It was then embraced by major cities such as Seattle, Las Vegas, and Pittsburgh who were among the early adopters. These innovators introduced branding to compete more effectively in an increasingly competitive world, create a strategic decision-making framework, and to address the calls on behalf of stakeholders for increased accountability in the marketing of places.

Most forward thinking places now regard branding as an essential component of their marketing toolkit. It has been elevated in importance to the point where the Destination Marketing Association International (DMAI), the world's largest official destination marketing organization, has designated the development of a brand strategy as one of the critical items needed for accreditation in the Association's "Destination Marketing Accreditation Program."

Malcolm Allan of *placebrands* in the UK maintains, "In the 21st century cities will increasingly compete on the value that they provide in terms of their physical, service and experiential offer, their heritage, their ambitions, and their character. In short: they will compete on their brand and will develop in line with it."

## Be Careful What You Wish For

While many places may have the *intention* of adopting a branded approach, they *unintentionally* fall short, opting instead for a superficial image "wrapper" in the form of a logo, tagline, or theme for an advertising campaign. In this book, we present a more holistic approach, showing how orchestrating, communicating and delivering a valued promise is the most important aspect of branding that any community must fulfill, irrespective of its size.

> **Many places unintentionally fall short of a brand strategy, opting instead for a logo, slogan, or theme for an advertising campaign.**

Too frequently, we see cities engage an agency to assist them in developing a brand strategy and the result is a slogan that provides no hint of a meaningful benefit or promised experience. These efforts are contributing nothing to the respect or relevance of the city among key audiences. In fact, some of these efforts are confusing and devalue the concept of destination branding.

The observation of Zeitgeist Consulting President Bill Geist was particularly relevant when he said, "There's an ocean of difference between a brand and a slogan. And, yet, we're seeing that body of water crossed with alarming regularity by firms that are jumping on the bandwagon and showering unsuspecting destination marketers with overblown promises of Nike-like brand awareness. Sure, every DMO pro dreams of developing a brand that resonates. But so many of the recent concepts we've seen from some of the 'brand-houses' out there are nothing more than catchy slogans that could be interchanged between destinations as easily as changing your shirt. Of course, after dropping $80,000 on a brand nobody wants to admit that what they're holding in their hand is a slogan ... so the dirty little secret continues to hide under wraps. But it's there all the same: these aren't brands."[2]

Whisper Brand Strategy Consultants expresses a similar sentiment: "Organizations are often sold a 'branding' service which is nothing more than, for example, advertising, public relations, or some other principle. The reason is that many design firms, pr groups, advertising agencies, research houses, architectural firms, and business consultants offer 'branding' services. But they do so from where they sit, so they can sell their core expertise – their logo design, pr, advertising, research, architecture, and business consulting services. Most of these firms will claim to be brand experts, but the reality is this: branding is a by-product of what they do."[3]

This should be a process aimed at doing more than making the participants in the process feel good about themselves. Those leading the effort need to clarify what they mean by 'branding' and their overall objectives. This will go a long way toward getting everyone onto the right page, making hard decisions, and recruiting the right kind of professional assistance.

## You've Got Company

In the USA there are approximately 20,000 cities, 3,400 counties, 126 America's Byways, and 12,800 designated National Historic Districts. That does not include the states, regions, resorts, and neighborhoods that are also clamoring for attention. No wonder most small and mid-sized cities find it hard to be seen and heard in this crowd!

It may be hard to believe that 90% of incorporated cities in the USA have a population of less than 50,000 residents.[4] Actually, 80% of them have less than 10,000 residents. That means that the struggle to gain attention is not limited to those with large populations and large marketing budgets. The "little guys" are also competing against other enterprising small cities in lower profile, but no less intense battles with the prizes being more family wage jobs, new businesses, high-spending travelers and affluent newcomers.

Today, cities of all sizes find themselves competing against places and organizations on the other side of the world. The global search for talented workers, advantageous conditions and access to markets has bought even small-town America onto the radar of global corporations. At the same time, international visitors to the USA have shown an increasing inclination to go beyond the traditional major gateway cities to discover more of the real America. This new paradigm means that ambitious communities have to compete by using the same principles that were once the exclusive domain of corporations and nations.

Destination choice is not limited to the battle between one city and another. Locations within cities are also in fierce competition with each other: city centers vs. neighborhoods, big box retailers vs. Main Streets, shopping malls vs. traditional downtowns, and suburbs competing with all of the above. We even find modern shopping centers in the suburbs that are built to look like traditional downtowns and Main Streets. Examples of this can be found at Bridgeport Village in Portland OR and The Streets at Southpoint in Durham NC. This heightened competitive environment makes it imperative for places, no matter their size or composition, to clearly differentiate themselves and to convey why they are relevant and highly valued options.

We've all had the experience of discovering that the reality of a place is different from the perceptions and expectations we hold. Those perceptions may have been shaped by our travel experiences, education, comments from friends and relatives, and even movies, books, songs, and television. A complex web of factors such as its distinctive location, geography, economy, climate, history, culture, religion or architecture has produced the city's actual character. The challenge for all ambitious communities is to bridge and manage the gap between the externally held perceptions and the reality of the place. Many are even trying to compete with an image that is out of date, inaccurate, or unbalanced.

To the annoyance of many city leaders, the commonly held view of their city may be out of step with what they see as its reality. While the city may have invested millions of dollars in infrastructure projects, public works, promotions, urban design, and events, an outdated or bland image may still be widely held after many years of positive change within the community.

Possibly the biggest challenge that many places face is having to reel in and manage a brand that has been unmanaged for a long time. "Most cities are victims of their unmanaged reputations," says Rod Underhill, chief executive of Spherical Inc. "In the absence of a brand strategy, the city may conjure images and associations that are not necessarily what the city would like to be known for. For instance, without a brand strategy the image of Dallas may have been limited to cultural icons such as J.R. Ewing and cheerleaders."[5]

Then there is the "blank slate" problem identified by Andy Levine, President of Development Counsellors International, who estimates that 60 to 70 percent of all cities in the U.S. have no dominant image at all in the public mind. Thus, finding a core differentiating asset, or 'unique selling proposition' as he terms it, becomes even more important.

Malcolm Allan of *placebrands* makes the point, "Competing on tax breaks, tax credits, free land, soft loans and other financial incentives to attract investors and to shore up local industries is clearly a race to the bottom and one that is impossible to sustain. What is needed is a frank rethink about what the city offers of value and will offer in future. City branding is about being distinctive and deliberately creating, developing and demonstrating that value through appropriate on-brand actions."

Fortunately, communities are becoming increasingly conscious of the need to proactively shape and influence what the world thinks of them and to position and market themselves with strategic intent. An important starting point is for city leaders to recognize that there is a direct link between the city's image and reputation, and its attractiveness as a place to visit, live, invest, and study. An even greater realization for some is that inaction is not a viable option if they genuinely want to improve local prosperity.

## CHAPTER ONE

# The World of Brands and Branding

## Over-Supply and Overload

We are living in the most over-communicated period in history. On an average day Americans are exposed to over 5,000 commercial messages in one way or another. These may be as subtle as the aroma from the Body Shop, a pop-up ad on a Website, the logo on a coffee cup, the placement of a soft drink can in a television show, or the livery of a FedEx van in the street. Our lives are cluttered with an over-abundance of products, advertising, media choices, marketing messages, and options. Products, whether they are coffee, automobiles, or cities somehow have to cut through this clutter and "noise" to connect with customers. We can be sure that this sensory overload is only going to intensify, heightening the need for all marketers to think beyond their traditional techniques and approaches.

The reaction of many consumers to this overload is to close down or try to block out these intrusions, as so many of us do with TiVo and pop-up blockers, in an effort to protect ourselves from this invasion of unwanted advertising. As marketers, this makes your task even more difficult and more expensive. Do you turn up the volume by placing more advertising? But what if you don't have a big advertising budget? Or should you play smarter and sharpen your messages to make it clear what you stand for? Take a leaf from the most successful marketers of consumer products who seem to be able to consistently demonstrate how they are distinctive, relevant, and meaningful by adopting a branded approach to their marketing. Branding is the most effective way to escape the sameness and blandness that has enveloped so many of your competitors.

It's easy to find look-alikes, clones and knock-offs of coffee, clothes, or even cities. Just take a look at the abundance of similar content in the brochures and Websites of various cities offering "me-too" physical features and characteristics. Winning destinations are increasingly those that are able to identify the special values, psychological needs, and desires that their customers hold most dear, and then connect those benefits and experiences to their customers, by providing irresistible reasons to think of the city as being different and representing greater value than the alternatives.

## What *IS* a Brand?

Branding has become a buzz word and is probably one of the most misunderstood concepts in business and tourism management today. There are probably as many definitions of a brand as there are branding books. There is no single definition. Marketers and academics are in agreement, however, that a brand is much more than a logo, tagline, or advertising theme. Playing around with a new logo on your business cards and stationery does not build a brand, nor will it gain any traction for you in the marketplace. And there are some who make the mistake of regarding their marketing as their brand. If you are going to develop a brand you'll quickly find that you need to adopt a strategic mindset, not just a promotional, tactical or short-term outlook. A true brand is an organizing principle that will influence everything you do as a DMO in order to orchestrate outstanding customer experiences.

> **Playing around with a new logo on your business cards and stationery does not build a brand, nor will it gain any traction for you in the marketplace.**

While there are many published definitions of a brand, the ones that you are most likely to see recognize that it contains several of the following elements:

- A name, sign, or symbol
- The source of a promise

- Distinctive or added value
- Personality and character
- The sum of the customer's thoughts and perceptions

A brand adds value, meaning and an invisible aura or spirit to a product or entity – even a generic product. Look in the produce section of your supermarket and you can see grapes, oranges, bananas, and tomatoes, all with stickers that proclaim a brand identity that offers superior, yet intangible points of difference. Even commodities as basic as water and salt have created powerful brands for Evian and Morton's, by promising intangible qualities that add value. We can consider a brand as being the difference between:

- A can of Coca Cola and a generic cola
- An amusement park and Disneyland
- An airline and Southwest Airlines
- A hotel and The Four Seasons

A brand is not a physical entity. It exists only in the customer's mind. A true brand must make and keep a clear, single-minded promise and then deliver on it. At times this is not an easy proposition for city leaders to understand or embrace.

Some branding experts suggest that the definition of a brand is best characterized as a collection of attitudes and perceptions in the mind of the consumer. I particularly like the definition provided by Janelle Barlow and Paul Stewart in *Branded Customer Service*, where they state "A brand is a metaphor for a complex pattern of associations that exists in the heads of individuals, not in the heads of the marketing department."[6]

Your community is not branded just because you say it is or because you stamp your logo on everything that leaves your office or paint it on the water tower and every blank wall around town. This is cosmetic branding. Actually, it's not even branding. It's like putting makeup on an aardvark: a veneer with no meaning, no customer relevance, and often without a hint of a promise that can be fulfilled.

## Our Lives Are Filled with Brands

So many everyday products occupy a special place in our hearts, minds and wallets. We don't buy a soft drink, we buy a Coke. We don't buy tissues, we buy Kleenex. We drink a Starbucks. Kids eat a Happy Meal. Even two and three-year-olds can identify the McDonald's logo and know what it stands for in their young minds.

Brands are ubiquitous. When churches, universities, stores, museums, celebrities, and sports teams are considered to be brands, you know brands have infiltrated just about every corner of our lives, and even our vocabulary. There are also plenty of books and audio programs advocating that each of us should present and manage *ourselves* as a brand to improve our career and business prospects.

In this era of super-brands it may seem an unusual notion to consider a city, state, region or country as a brand. However, in the context of a *place* selling itself as a focal point to visit or to buy real estate, it makes sense that it should be managed as a brand to shape and control its identity and to make choices easier for customers.

**Another way to consider the most effective brands is to think of them as capsules of valuable information.**

We seem to be "pre-wired" to accept information in the way that brands interact with us. Brands make it easy for us to recall and prefer brands by the way that we consider, store and retrieve information. The most effective have the ability to pre-sell themselves because they allow us to be loyal and predisposed toward their benefits and perceived extra value. They have the ability to short circuit and speed up our consideration and buying decisions. Some of the reasons we may have a preference for branded products over unbranded products is because they:

- Add to our self esteem
- Create stronger images and perceptions
- Increase awareness
- Improve our knowledge
- Increase trust and loyalty
- Simplify decisions
- Stimulate feelings
- Tap into past experiences

Another way to consider the most effective brands is to think of them as capsules of valuable information. Brands make our buying decisions easier by doing a lot of the thinking for us. They aim directly at our hearts, and then satisfy our logic. Great brands first tap into our emotions because they drive and initiate most, if not all, of our decisions and then provide the logic for us to rationalize our decision. Newport RI, San Diego North CA, and Kissimmee FL each do a great job in engaging our senses and then confirming our feelings through the logic of their excellent brochures, packages and Websites. The recently launched Website by Sault St. Marie in Northern Ontario, Canada is very much attuned to conveying experiences and emotion rather than focusing simply on the physical characteristics of the city.

## What Is a Destination Brand?

A destination is a place that gains relevance because of its power to entice people to leave one location in order to visit or relocate to another. Destinations include many types of geographical entities such as countries, cities, neighborhoods, malls, museums, theme parks, and a variety of other places.

**A destination brand is the totality of perceptions, thoughts, and feelings that customers hold about a place.**

After years of branding places of all sizes, the following mantra has evolved to guide our destination brand planning:

– 25 –

*__A destination brand__ is the totality of perceptions, thoughts, and feelings that customers hold about a place.*

*__Destination branding__ is an organizing principle that involves orchestrating the messages and experiences associated with the place to ensure that they are as distinctive, compelling, memorable, and rewarding as possible. Successful destination brands reside in the customer's heart and mind, clearly differentiate themselves, deliver on a valued promise, and simplify customer choices.*

*The brand's value is built at every point of contact with customers through exceptional experiences, not by relying on the physical characteristics of the place alone. Each experience before, during and after the visit has a vital role in defining and delivering the promise that is inherent within the brand.*

Unless a brand is adopted, supported and given "life" by stakeholders and partners at each critical point of contact with customers, it will amount to nothing more than a logo or tagline on a piece of paper. Partners throughout the destination, whether it is a city or Main Street, must embrace the attitude that *every time* they are in touch with a customer is an opportunity to positively reinforce and build the brand through customer experiences.

In essence, the hallmark of a successful destination brand is determined by the promises that it makes, and the promises that it keeps. Despite their good faith and good intentions, communities can find this challenging because it takes passion, commitment, innovation and, most importantly a lot of collaborative behavior to sustain the on-brand behavior that is required.

## It's About Your Good Name

After implementing your current marketing plan, what is it that you hope to have built? In addition to a healthy flow of new business, your answer should include "our brand equity." All marketing actions should work toward building a strong and meaningful brand image and accurately position the place in the minds of customers.

The decision to visit or invest in a place is based on faith and trust because customers are purchasing an intangible. In this situation, image and reputation are highly influential in relocation, investment or travel decisions. It is this image and the customer's trust in the experiences associated with the place that are the real product customers are buying.

Over time, a successful brand adds to its own value and reputation by consistently satisfying its customers. This value is referred to as brand equity, and is its accumulated loyalty, awareness, and financial value. I like to think of it as owning a piggy bank, or a bank account, in the minds of your target audience. Good news, enticing images, and positive experiences are deposits in the bank. But bad news, poor marketing efforts, and sub-standard experiences are therefore withdrawals from the community's account. To be strong and resilient, a brand must have sufficient equity on deposit for when those bad things happen. And bad weather, a natural disaster, a scandal or bad experiences do happen from time to time, even to good places.

Many brands are juggernauts within the global economy. It is estimated that 70% of McDonalds $26 billion market value, and 50% of Coca Cola's $68 billion worth, is their brand value. Considered another way, if Coke lost everything except its formula and brand identity those intangibles alone could still be sold for billions and billions of dollars. It is little wonder that Coke and McDonalds undertake such strenuous efforts to protect the integrity and value of their good names.

To be honest, many city leaders don't understand the benefits and concepts involved in place branding (or marketing for that matter!). Some are simply uncomfortable in using the term "branding" or even "marketing" and the city's name in the same sentence. We have found that when city officials think in terms of their city's image or reputation rather than its brand, they are more likely to "get it." While this is certainly not technically an accurate description of a brand or branding, we have found that it does enable many to better understand and support the concept and its benefits.

Who is responsible, and what is the plan for building and protecting the good name of your city? The thoughts and associations that come to mind when your city's name is heard or read are likely to have huge financial, political, and social value. Just think for a moment about the number of jobs, businesses, and other organizations that have a stake in its image and reputation. Unfortunately, it is a value that goes largely unrecognized and unappreciated. And perhaps most importantly, unprotected. It rarely gets measured, and never appears on a balance sheet or the job evaluation of a Chamber President, City Manager or Mayor. The level of esteem that a city's name evokes with key audiences has a direct impact on the health of its tourism, economic development, prestige, and respect. With so much riding on its image, doesn't it make sense to have a plan to cultivate, manage, and protect this most valuable of city assets?

**When city officials think in terms of their city's image or reputation rather than its brand, they are more likely to "get it."**

Proud and ambitious cities must nurture and protect their good names, the same as Coca Cola and Nike protect their names and use strong brand management principles to sustain their distinctive image. While many leaders may sign-on for improving the city image, they need to be reminded that it must be more than an exercise in "polishing." If there isn't a concerted campaign involving all key elements of the community the effort will fall short of their desired objectives.

While community and civic leaders may debate and procrastinate over the issue of branding, those who actively value their city image soon recognize that if they are serious about their city's vision, developing a brand identity is really not an option.

Every time a person interacts with the city they are deriving thoughts and building perceptions about the place. A community that does not proactively engage in managing these encounters will be positioned anyway, but by its customers, competitors, and the media – probably to its disadvantage. It may well be tagged with attributes and an image that it doesn't want.

## Is It Time for a Destination Brand?

A well-conceived brand strategy can provide increased effectiveness and efficiency for all of the city's marketing efforts. It sets the guidelines for how the city should be described, depicted, and behave in regard to target audiences. If individual tactical decisions are driving marketing programs, then it is time for the intervention and strategic discipline of a brand strategy.

A quick test to assess your city's brand readiness is to consider:

- Is it well known?
- Is the image accurate?
- Is it highly regarded?
- Do target audiences care what the city stands for or what it can do for them?
- How different is the city from others?

The imbalance between the internal identity and the external image of many places limits its development. This often happens when the city is projecting itself as one thing, but the reality is far different. For example, the city promotes itself as a place for romantic beach getaways, but visitors find that restaurant service is a nightmare, hotels are substandard, and that after-hour beach walkways are hard to find and poorly lit. Strong, successful brands don't display this kind of dissonance. City marketers must constantly monitor customer satisfaction and "test drive" their own experiences to ensure that they are of a high standard and are aligned with the promises that they are making.

If there is a gap between the reality of your city and the views that outsiders hold about it, then you need a strategy to bridge this gap. Whether people hold an overly positive or negative image, you must address the situation since both of these scenarios can cause problems. An overly positive one can lead to customer disappointment, while a negative image will lead potential customers to spend their time and money elsewhere and possibly perpetuate negative word of mouth.

**If individual tactical decisions are driving marketing programs, then it is time for the intervention and strategic discipline of a brand strategy.**

When individual tactical decisions are driving marketing programs, it's time for the intervention and strategic discipline of a brand strategy in order to coordinate those disparate activities and make the most of your scarce marketing resources.

The Websites and brochures of your city's various messengers may look great, but without a brand strategy it will be a matter of luck as to whether there is cohesion and consistency in their look, story, and message. So often, the "ad of the month" syndrome is at play where marketers constantly change their communications in the hope of finding a message that will strike the right chord. Brand planning is the ideal way to avoid this kind of marketing schizophrenia where there is no consistency or clarity to the way the place presents itself.

It may be time to develop a brand strategy when you detect one or more of the following conditions:

- The need to overcome a dated, confusing, or inaccurate image.
- New infrastructure developments or a major event are likely to redefine the place.
- A downtown or cultural revitalization program is being launched.
- The overall marketing messages of the city and its partners lack focus or differentiation.

- A need for greater ROI from marketing.
- Constantly changing advertising messages and themes.
- A lack of unity and consistency in the communications of city messengers.
- A competitor has a disproportionate "share of mind."
- Traditional markets are declining in size and value.
- Marketing resources are being applied in an inefficient or un-coordinated manner.

## Branding Cities Calls for a Different Approach

The path to revealing a community-based brand usually involves a multitude of stakeholders and may depart somewhat from that generally followed for branding corporate products and services. One reason for the variation is the composite nature of communities which are a compilation of many independent and competing businesses, products, and experiences that may be owned and managed by many different organizations with no single management team or brand custodian.

Additionally, unlike a consumer product such as a soft drink, cities are not discrete or independent entities. A city is much more complex and cannot be reformulated or terminated if it is not popular or is under-performing. Nor can it introduce different products under different names, as Black and Decker has done with its DeWalt line of tools.

> **A city brand must be able to stand the test of time, public debate, political scrutiny, media questions, and the analysis of marketing partners.**

Cities generally have extremely limited marketing budgets compared to the marketing resources of many consumer and service brands. Exacerbating the situation is the pressure from city stakeholders and the challenge of developing a simple positioning message that will resonate with customers yet capture the city's diverse attributes.

While a corporate brand may need approval by a marketing team or Board, the city brand may require endorsement by the City Council and other organizations in which political players may never see eye-to-eye. A problem for many city brands is that some important leaders frequently do not have strong marketing credentials, nor do they have a customer-focused perspective, yet they can exert considerable influence over the process. This is stressed by authors Nigel Morgan and Annette Pritchard who point out, "If a city brand is to be developed as a coherent entity, participants in the process must be aware of the potentially destructive role of politics."[7] The city brand must overcome enmity and rise above politics. The support of the political leaders in small cities is vital and must be nurtured because it is important to gain their endorsement and understanding of the branding assignment.

Community-based brands often must withstand a level of political and public debate that consumer brands rarely have to undergo. A city brand has to be able to stand the test of time, public debate, political scrutiny, media questions, and the analysis of marketing partners. The best way to insulate the brand from this scrutiny is to generate community and partner buy-in and involvement from the start through an open consultative process.

For most cities, the challenge is to orchestrate cohesive brand messages and experiences through the commitment of many local players, including neighborhoods, attractions, hotels, tours, real estate agents, and restaurants that may also be competitors to each other. Brand planning for cities usually requires an approach that is more conciliatory and inclusive than that found in the branding of most consumer products. For instance, being very specific with the positioning may unintentionally alienate many groups and cause controversy. Conversely, the trick is to not dilute the positioning to the point where the place loses its strongest competitive edge and ends up being seen as meaningless or irrelevant.

## True Brands Don't Belong Only to the Marketing Department

Branding is often mistakenly regarded as just another word for marketing or advertising, and "belongs in the marketing department." In fact, it needs to be far more pervasive. The brand should first and foremost be regarded as a strategic discipline and be the central organizing and decision-making principle for the DMO and its partners influencing everything that they do.

While a strong brand has many benefits for customers (including making their buying decisions much easier), it should also make internal decision making clearer for the Board, staff, marketers, vendors, and stakeholders because all actions are filtered according to their likely effect on the brand. At the heart of a true city brand is a unifying movement that results in hundreds and sometimes thousands of actions coming into alignment at critical moments during the customer's encounters with the place. To aid this alignment, destination marketers should constantly ask themselves:

- Will this action help or hurt the brand?
- How can this best enhance the brand?

From the outset it's usually necessary to encourage the DMO Board and community leaders to embrace the rewards of a healthy city brand. The realization that it can mean increased income, jobs, profitability, respect and community well-being can spark a revolution, even among skeptics.

If the management and advocacy for the brand is confined to the folks in the DMO's marketing department, it's unlikely to reach the level of potency expected. However, when leaders get past the notion that a brand will simply bring a change to the color scheme or a snappy new slogan they may be more willing to remove impediments and introduce the type of thinking, resources and cooperation that will empower brand building and challenge the community to achieve its greatest potential.

The more community branding assignments that I work on, the more I recognize that they are also an exercise in change management. To achieve success, the destination must move beyond the resistance of some individuals and organizations. A success-

> **A genuine mandate for branding success may require a change of mindset within, and between, many organizations.**

ful community brand may require changes to regulations, laws, systems, budgets, processes, resources, and recruitment. Above all, it may call for a change of attitude. The first casualty may be the old "that's the way we've always done it around here" attitude. A genuine mandate for branding success may require a change of mindset within, and between, many organizations. It may involve the need to overcome individual disagreements and turf protection. Tearing down unhelpful barriers, attitudes, and processes can be major steps forward. Collaboration, networking, integration, and co-operation are the signatures of healthy brand planning. This certainly takes more than the efforts of the DMO alone – it should be everybody's business!

## Planning for Community-Based Brands

By adopting the principles of branding, you are introducing a more strategically focused approach to your marketing. Branding should provide the strategic and decision-making framework to better orchestrate the messages and experiences emanating from the place. It should be strategic (not tactical) and approached with a long-term view.

The overall process for formulating a brand strategy is much the same irrespective of the destination's size. However, individual elements and emphasis will vary according to the available budget, the size of the city, stage of development, market sophistication, complexity of its economic base, and the accuracy of its existing image in external markets. Each place brings its own relationships, politics, history, and attitudes.

Chambers of Commerce and CVBs are usually the best situated organizations within the community to plan, coordinate, and manage the branding process. They generally have strong relationships with a wide cross-section of other organizations and are, themselves, the most committed to the marketing of the city. Their mandate and their tourism-related constituents have a strong, direct influence on the overall image and marketing activities. In some cases, the mayor's office or another overarching entity may be in the best position to lead the effort, especially if they embrace the need to nurture and protect the city's image.

One thing is for sure: there is no "silver bullet" or one-size-fits-all solution that will quickly deliver a sustainable brand strategy. While there are several generic brand planning processes for consumer and service brands, all usually contain the following steps:

- Situation Assessment and Analysis
- Defining the Brand
- Brand Communication
- Managing the Brand

Decades of working with countries, cities and regions has led us to create our highly successful *7A Destination Branding Process*. The *7A Process* had its genesis during my years of international branding for Australia and other countries, and later evolved through tourism marketing and strategic planning assignments for communities in Australia and the USA. This led me to formulate an approach that is a blend of community planning disciplines, the analytical techniques used in tourism planning, and the strong integrated marketing and brand planning principles learned from working with some of the world's leading destinations.

As the name implies, the *7A Destination Branding Process* leads cities through seven steps to encourage thoroughness and to ensure that important voices are not overlooked or minimized. This system is explained in more detail in Chapter 5.

## Branding: It's Not Just for the Big Guys

When great brands come to mind, we often think of the high profile advertising that accompanies them. However, big budget advertising campaigns are not always the common factor in great brands. Starbucks, Google, The Body Shop, Krispy Kreme, and Tupperware were established with little or no advertising. Their outstanding customer experiences are what generated the extreme loyalty among their millions of global customers.

**Branding is all about organizing, differentiation and focus. A large budget should not be a prerequisite for harnessing these forces.**

Cities of all sizes often labor over the decision to develop a brand strategy. For small ambitious cities it is increasingly becoming a matter of whether they can afford *not* to embrace the concept so that they can focus and organize their marketing efforts. If the DMO allocates funds to marketing campaigns without clarifying what the city offers, what it does best, and why it matters to customers, it is risking public funds. No matter the city's size, a formalized brand framework can channel the energies and resources of marketing partners to orchestrate the best results from their combined investments, however limited. Branding is all about organizing, differentiation and focus. And a large budget is not needed to harness these forces. If a city is *not* differentiated, it is bland – and bland places are often left to compete solely on lower price points. Those that are focused and differentiated, and can strike an emotional chord are able to mobilize their marketing resources with greater effect. These attributes are even more important if the city does not have a large marketing budget.

It is amazing how some places may take great care of their streets, parks and buildings, yet have totally dropped the ball when it comes to their external image. Even without a large budget, a city can have an Internet presence that defies its size. The Internet has opened a world for more than just the big guys!

The online world is a great equalizer. One of my favorite cartoons was in an early edition of *The Internet for Dummies*. The cartoon showed two dogs working at a computer, and one dog said to the other, *"I love the Internet. No one knows that you're a dog."* Just like that dog, the Internet enables places of all sizes to present themselves attractively and reach prospects worldwide in a very cost-effective manner. They are able to make very strong statements through the look, style, and content of their Web presence. The size of the place doesn't matter when it comes to an innovative online branding and marketing strategy that provides attractive designs and navigation, plus search engine optimization and clever linking. The Websites of small cities such as Carlsbad CA, Newport RI and Huntington Beach CA creatively present their enticing and motivational content which strongly convey their sense of place and the experiences that they promise.

## CHAPTER TWO

# The Challenges and Rewards of Branding Places

## Hey! Look at Us!

It's not easy for small cities to attract positive attention, but it *is* easy to forget that the rest of the world is not as interested in our hometown as those of us who live there. Small cities generally have rare opportunities to capture our attention or to impress the outside world.

Each year, thousands of small places across the USA come to the forefront in the national media for a few seconds in news reports or other events, and then disappear from our radar again. We usually don't spend much time thinking about cities other than those that are regularly covered in the media, or those where we live, have visited, do business in, or where friends and relatives live. When we do hear of them, it is often for the wrong reasons such as bad weather, disasters, crime, accidents, or maybe in a more positive vein, for sporting events, famous people, or travelogues. Additionally, the media often unknowingly reinforces negative stereotypes or conveys inaccurate and outdated information about places.

Cities wanting to maintain or elevate the standard of living of their residents must counter unproductive stereotypes about themselves. This is more of a challenge for those that have not actively projected a contemporary image of themselves or have not had a flow of visitors to see the reality of what the place is really like. Outdated and inaccurate images frequently prove slow and difficult to eradicate, even in the minds of residents who don't recognize the positive changes that have occurred around them.

This is a real dilemma for places wanting to reach out and influence people in a very crowded and noisy world full of negative or indifferent media coverage. Changing the city's image for the long term requires a well planned and systematic approach that goes beyond a quick fix advertising campaign, no matter how creative the campaign may be.

## What are the Benefits of a Strong Community Brand?

While a brand strategy may be initiated with a clear set of objectives, we have found that the process often brings many unexpected bonuses, even before the brand is launched. The benefits for both your customers and your community may include:

### THE BENEFITS FOR YOUR CUSTOMER

1. Provides peace of mind by increasing trust and confidence.
2. Saves time and effort.
3. Simplifies choices.
4. Associations with the place reflects well on them.
5. Taps into their needs and desires.
6. Provides perceived added value and benefits.

### THE BENEFITS FOR YOUR COMMUNITY'S MARKETERS

1. Provides a greater strategic focus.
2. Fosters a unified and cooperative approach to city marketing.
3. Establishes a clear, valued, and sustainable point of distinction in the minds of customers.
4. Provides a decision-making framework to build a strong, consistent brand identity and avoid contradictory and changing designs, messages, and images.
5. Results in a higher return on investment (ROI) from marketing investments.
6. Enables premium pricing rather than relying on discounts and incentives.
7. Introduces a more persuasive and efficient way to communicate with customers.

8.  Leads to improved partnerships, distribution and publicity.
9.  Creates a deterrent to competitors wanting to introduce similar messages, products, and experiences: the "first mover" advantage.
10. Provides an umbrella to capture the character and personality of the city enabling all marketers to use similar consistent and compelling messages.
11. Generates loyalty through more repeat customers and word-of-mouth referrals.
12. Provides a distinctive look and feel for marketing applications.

## THE BENEFITS FOR YOUR COMMUNITY AS A WHOLE

1.  Creates a unifying focus for all public, private, and non-profit sector organizations that rely on the image of the place and its attractiveness.
2.  Brings increased respect, recognition, loyalty, and celebrity.
3.  Corrects out of date, inaccurate or unbalanced perceptions.
4.  Improves stakeholder revenues, profit margins, and increases lodging tax revenues.
5.  Increases the attractiveness of local products.
6.  Increases the ability to attract, recruit, and retain talented people.
7.  Provides the foundation for future product development, new businesses and investment.
8.  Enhances civic pride and advocacy.
9.  Allows a faster recovery if the place is affected by a crisis, such as a natural disaster or bad publicity.
10. Results in a lower turnover rate of businesses in prime locations.
11. Expands the size of the pie for stakeholders to get a larger share, rather than having to rely on pricing to steal share.
12. Contributes toward a broader economic base.

A place that has a healthy and respected brand identity can be a catalyst for leaders, businesses, and citizens being welcomed in the "right circles," gaining seats on the "right" committees, attracting awards and grants, winning bids to host events, and attracting conferences and meetings. It makes it easier for a place (and its citizens) to be selected in any competitive setting because it is seen to have qualities and benefits that are good to be associated with.

## How Do Places Get Their Image?

Why are we drawn to some places more than others? There are some that seem to get more attention than others. They win bids for major events and are less affected by the fallout from unfortunate events and can quickly bounce back from setbacks. Some cities just seem to have a Teflon-like positive aura surrounding them. We tend to ignore their blemishes and keep a special place for them in our hearts. We feel great loyalty toward them – without necessarily having lived there, nor even visited there.

A city's image can be considered to evolve in three sequential stages. The first is the *organic image* that is formed by our general awareness of the place through influences such as media coverage, books, movies, family and friends, and educational studies. This organic image is even more potent if the city has a long, interesting history, distinctive cultural fabric, outstanding natural wonders, or is a major population, business or political center.

The second stage is formed by the *marketing induced* image which as its name infers, is mainly shaped by marketing communications, such as advertising, public relations, Websites, brochures and sales presentations. That is, it is built through promotional messages in addition to the organic image or basic awareness of the place.

The third stage is the *experiential* phase where the image is enhanced by the person's first-hand encounters. Every community that attracts leisure or business travelers will experience this stage.

While some destinations may be able to skip the second stage, i.e. marketing communications, no city can avoid the third. This is, as they say, "where the rubber hits the road." To sustain a positive *organic* or *marketing induced* image, the place has to live up to its promises in the *experiential* phase.

All cities may not be as handsomely endowed or as distinctive as say, historic St. Augustine FL, Nantucket MA, or Santa Fe NM. Each has a compelling organic image and has nurtured a strong and distinctive identity that has evolved from their colorful origins. For them, it is somewhat easier to fulfill each phase.

Over the decades, and in many cases centuries, the influences of history, famous (and infamous) people, events, culture and arts, geography, politics, sports, entertainment and celebrities have all contributed toward building the persona and image of places. On the other hand, our love for a place may stem from something as simple as our childhood memories of visiting Grandma. An image that has evolved over decades or centuries may have little or no relevance in the reality of today's economy or tourism needs. This syndrome most noticeably impacted cities that were referred to as post-industrial or being in the "Rustbelt." The renaissance of Pittsburgh, formerly the home of Big Steel, has been amazing. The city has reinvented itself as a center for excellence in technology, culture and sports. This inspirational story has been replicated in other post-industrial centers around the world such as Buffalo NY, Cleveland OH, Birmingham in England, and Newcastle, my hometown in Australia.

When a city has a negative image that has evolved over decades, it's very difficult, if not impossible, to change it in the short term. This is very common for cities that have long-held industrial images and unlike consumer products, an extended advertising campaign will rarely do the trick. Even with a concerted effort, it may still take 15 to 20 years to fully leave behind their outdated industrial image. This has been the case for cities like Tacoma WA and Milwaukee WI, which after long associations as industrial cities are now being recognized as important cultural centers.

## Is It an Image Problem or Reality?

The terms *image* and *identity* are often confused. Brand *image* relates to how the brand is perceived from the customer's point of view, while brand *identity* is the unique set of visual, auditory and other stimuli that express the brand and shape its image. Each must be deeply rooted in the strategic foundations of the brand. Think of brand identity as being like the identity of a friend, comprised of his or her name, appearance, personality, vocabulary, speech, ethnicity, and style of dress among many other elements. Image, on the other hand, comes from the external view. It is what people really think of the place. It is their perceptions .... and their reality.

**Cities often have a reality problem that city leaders prefer not to recognize.**

Sometimes we hear that a city has an "image problem." Actually, they often have a "reality problem" that city leaders prefer not to recognize. The real issue is that their image does not match the way that they would like to be perceived. Too often, the statements *"We need a new logo"* or *"Let's develop a brand"* is the cover for deeper and more troubling problems. Sooner or later the underlying issues must addressed.

We were once invited to develop a city's brand strategy, and were told that the mayor had already determined that he wanted the city to be known as a regional center for the arts. This may not necessarily be a problem, as long as the resources are being deployed to ensure that this vision can be a reality and the promise can be delivered. In this case, the mayor's mindset did not match the reality of the community's cultural assets. He did not realize that the brand or image was not what *he* said it was, but rather what *customers* said it was. We declined the assignment because the mayor was inflexible and the city did not have the capacity to fulfill the mayor's vision. Since then, my observations of this city have validated our assessment because they have still not developed the necessary cultural assets to justify its claim of being a center for the arts.

Strong brands are built on trust. There must be alignment between what the city's brand promises and the reality of the actual experience. If the two are out of sync the brand will not be sustainable unless there are plans and resources to bridge the gap. If the city's performance is of a high standard and its image is bad or non-existent, then it has an inadequate brand or image strategy and may need increased or more accurate communications. For instance, the hundreds of interviews conducted during the brand planning process for Toledo OH. revealed that "the city didn't have a negative image – it simply had no image at all."[8] Toledo's long term brand strategy was then designed to address this situation.

Every city's image is formed by customers' exposure to the accumulated experiences and knowledge of the place. These impressions or associations may be positive, negative, or neutral. In the case of Las Vegas, the image of it may be "a great place where adults are free to do anything they want, whenever they want." This is right in line with the identity that is projected by the Las Vegas Convention and Visitors Authority, and is captured by their tagline *What happens here, stays here*™.

If a city has a negative or neutral image, some city leaders and marketers may like to jump to an advertising or publicity-based solution. This tactic may only serve to make their situation worse, as attracting more visitors before the root cause of the problem has been addressed may generate negative word of mouth. Additionally, an advertising based solution is likely to have only a superficial effect in improving the city's image unless it is matched by a concerted effort to deliver outstanding experiences.

Kerrie Walters, Executive Director of Grants Pass OR Visitors and Convention Bureau, put it well when she said, "Branding a community involves many balancing acts. For example, the brand has to match-up with the community's self image, yet not be limited by it. It needs to be shaped by its strengths, while stretching them, without becoming contrived and losing its authenticity. What we project to outside audiences must be true to the reality of who and what we are. This has been our challenge in making the Grants Pass brand sustainable."

A city has a real image challenge when people outside of the city do not accurately know the reality of the place. We see evidence of this when city leaders say:

- "People don't know how good our new waterfront redevelopment is."
- "People assume that because we are a small city, we don't have any good restaurants."
- "Relocation agents don't think of us as being easily accessible, despite the quality of our airport and interstate freeways" and so on.

## Partnerships – You've Gotta Have Friends!

Successful destination brands are all about cooperative marketing, partnerships and alliances because their effectiveness depends upon collaborative relationships. Partners may come together for one-off activities or for long-term programs. Without partnerships, formalized or not, the marketing of any city is seriously weakened. Almost always, the organization that is responsible for the marketing of the destination does not own or manage the key brand components.

Cooperative partnerships are not limited to relationships within the city, but often extend to the cooperation and alliances between cities as well. They are strengthened by collaborating with nearby cities and locations to make the general region more appealing and meaningful. These partnerships may also take the form of byways, touring routes, as regional and historic themes such as Civil War Trails, or simple geographic identities such as The Adirondacks and The Outer Banks NC.

Some of the benefits of working in partnerships are:

- A bigger 'pie' for everyone to get larger slices
- Increased ROI from marketing investments
- Increased customers, increased income, and increased tax revenues
- It may give your story more meaning
- More opportunities to reach new markets
- More power, interest and message coverage
- The prospect of greater respect and credibility

Collaboration may take the form of a marketing plan or one-off activities such as a joint trade mission, trade show exhibit, a Website, brochure, sales calls, or hosting media visits. All will provide more cost-effective ways to reach and influence markets than if the partners attempted to do it by themselves. When you are considering the level of resources to invest in any partnership, think about:

- Are your target markets compatible?
- Are the partnership's strategies compatible with yours, or do they distract from your strategic focus?
- Are there shared values, goals and a commitment to quality between the organizations?
- Will it open new markets or difficult to reach niches?
- What is their history of successful relationships and results?
- Would it be more profitable to act alone or with a different partner?
- Will your major competitors be involved in the relationship?
- Is building this new dimension of your brand better than going alone?
- Will the resulting financial savings enable you to expand other marketing programs?
- Will it give you access to improved exposure, technology, expertise, logistics and resources?
- Does this relationship make sense, or is it happening because of politics and tradition?

## CHAPTER THREE

# What Is Being Branded and Why?

From the outset you need to gain agreement on the type of brand, exactly what is being branded and who is the target audience. Is this to be the overarching brand for all marketing efforts on behalf of the city? Is it from a tourism or economic development perspective, or is the goal to reposition or totally reinvent the identity of the city? What are the boundaries? Is it just the downtown and city center, or the entire city? There is a delicate balance in the geographical, partner and political scope of a community-based brand. If the brand tries to cover too wide an area, it may become diluted by relying on weak points of commonality in order to gain agreement among stakeholders.

Everyone should be clear about the parameters of the assignment, that you are solving the right problem, and not ignoring the underlying issues. Without this clarity, the exercise can quickly descend into confusion, ambiguity and controversy. Some so-called branding efforts result in nothing more than exercises in getting new designs for local police cars, stationery, and community pride.

Cities don't have the flexibility of a corporation when it comes to expanding or pruning their products. They may have boundaries that are the result of legislation and relationships that have been in place for many years. They are geographic entities that have "hot spots" or clusters which are of greater significance to visitors and new businesses than other areas within the city. Unlike commercial entities, in one way or another cities usually have to accommodate their weaker product elements.

## What Is the Objective?

On one level, stakeholders can agree that their primary goal is to increase visitation, attract newcomers, maximize investment, win major events, improve the image, or some other outcome that is commercially oriented. But there are other dynamics that underpin these performance measures that need to be considered. Like consumer products, cities have a lifecycle where their popularity may rise and fall over time. Their image may also become tired and need to be rejuvenated in some way.

The owners and managers of consumer brands have a number of options for addressing their product's performance. They can revitalize or reposition it, milk it for revenue, sell it off, or kill it off. On the other hand, community leaders and destination marketers have fewer and different options because they certainly can't sell the city or kill it off. They have to consider whether their strategies should involve:

1. Repositioning,
2. Reinventing, or
3. Doing nothing and maintaining the status quo (and possibly the downward spiral).

## Repositioning: Change the Way They See Us

The world in which any brand lives is dynamic. There are many forces that constantly influence demand – customer needs, trends, competitors, and the broad political, economic and social environments. Over the years, these forces can have a profound impact on the positioning and image of a city.

The majority of city branding efforts involve repositioning, or more specifically realigning, the positioning and brand identity. In many cases there may have been no obvious positioning and it is really a matter of bringing clarity to its identity by defining what the city stands for, how it is presented and the markets that it targets.

A city wanting to reposition itself will have to either modify the way that customers think about it or start targeting new markets. This means that it may need to redefine its relationship with customers and what they think of the place relative to competitors. In order to achieve this, it's preferable to make careful, incremental refinements rather than attempt to take the potentially risky and expensive step to a new market position in one move.

Changing what a city stands for in the customer's mind can be a challenging and expensive proposition. Las Vegas learned this in the early 1990s when it attempted to reposition the city as a place for family entertainment. After several years, they recognized that it was not appropriate and redefined their positioning as the city for adult freedom.

Changing perceptions can be a long-term proposition. Even then, there is no guarantee of success. It can be made even more difficult, as Las Vegas discovered, when it must balance the tasks of attracting new markets and changing its image while retaining current customers. Las Vegas was able to successfully recapture its prized position in large part through dramatic infrastructure developments, exciting new entertainment and its award-winning *What happens here, stays here*™ campaign.

When a city has significant new infrastructure, hallmark events, or cultural investments that represent major changes, then repositioning through marketing communications should become a priority. If the changes are not conveyed to external markets a gap may form between its image and reality. Repositioning may also be necessary when a city decides that it's time to correct long-held negative images. Specific changes such as crime reduction, expanded parking, and improved cleanliness may be important stimulants for changing the way that people think about a place.

Repositioning or revitalizing a city's image may be centered on the way that it projects itself in marketing communications, appearance, and its actual customer experiences. Consider the story of New

York City during the 1970s when just about everyone had written it off because of deteriorating infrastructure, crime, and financial problems. Not even President Ford would come to the aid of New York City with federal financial aid, prompting the New York Daily News front page headline "Ford to New York: Drop Dead." Leaders had to engineer the city's path back to prosperity and building a strong brand identity was integral to that vision. Interestingly, it was during these darkest days that the State's famed *I Love New York* campaign was born and over the next decade played an important role in the city's renaissance. It tapped into the city's reservoir of goodwill and rallied support by boosting, not competing with, the city's identity as "the Big Apple." It was the catalyst for significant growth in its tourism economy, as well as in boosting investment and enhancing its attractiveness and celebrity. The renaissance of New York, both City and State, was remarkable. Unfortunately, for every New York there are hundreds of cities of all sizes that don't recover from their setbacks. Too many walk the tightrope between life and oblivion, hoping for rescue by divine intervention.

For a long time, the area in downtown Seattle that is home to Pike Place Market and the Seattle Art Museum did not have a clear identity or name of its own even though people thought of it as distinct from other parts of downtown. Over time this nameless neighborhood became known for independent businesses, culture, diversity and the arts. Leaders felt it was time to refocus the way that people felt about it. The Downtown Seattle Association, building on the area's renaissance, repositioned the neighborhood by introducing a new name, logo, tagline and more precise messages to change perceptions, drive foot traffic and develop even more awareness of the area. The neighborhood with no name is now known as West Edge and has become one of Seattle's most vibrant commercial and visitor areas.

Another distinctive area in Seattle, the Chinatown International District, conducted public surveys and discovered that it was perceived as having sidewalks and street conditions that were a turn-off for visitors. A concerted image improvement process was initiated which included removing graffiti and litter, and establishing public art and beautification projects. The introduction of customer incentives and increased promotion resulted in a healthy revitalization for the area with visitors returning to the district and many new businesses being established.

Even long established destinations need to periodically refresh their offerings to sustain their popularity and relevance. "Waikiki is in the position of being at once Hawaii's most visited destination and the part of the state that has been most out of sync with visitor perceptions of the 'idyllic Hawaiian vacation'. After initial research, Hawaii Visitors & Convention Bureau (HVCB) realized that Waikiki should be positioned to convey a more modern and evolving interpretation of the spirit of Aloha – a beachfront melting pot in which Western and Polynesian combine to create the 'Waikiki Phenomenon'. The VCB focused on the idea that the experience of Aloha isn't locked in the past, but rather a living and breathing entity that shapes a unique culture and lifestyle in Waikiki." The repositioning is being supported by a US $1 billion revitalization of the city.[9]

## Reinventing: Take a Second Lease on Life

Reinvention of a community is a planned transformation that may take the form of new infrastructure, major events, business incentives, or possibly retail and residential developments. They often represent a radical departure from the past and directly impact the image and character of the location. These programs may occur over a long period such as those involving Bricktown – Oklahoma City, The Pearl District – Portland OR and Baltimore Harbor – Baltimore MD.

The redevelopment of New York City's Times Square transformed it from an area better known for crime, peep shows and winos to one of the city's most popular visitor attractions with Disney, Sony and the Virgin mega store, theater productions, and theme restaurants now attracting millions of visitors a week, including families.

Strategies to reinvent a city or sections of it are expensive, but the financial commitment is often necessary to inject new life to the area by attracting visitors, residents, sports fans, conference delegates, shoppers, students, or investors. In these situations the "brand team" is just as likely to be a team of architects and developers who may be totally focused on their developments and not on branding. Visionary city leaders may also decide to stimulate major private and public infrastructure projects to totally redefine the city. These projects rarely have the principles of overall city branding in mind when they are initiated. It is often a case where city marketers must play "catch-up" with the city leaders, investors, developers, and entrepreneurs and realign or reposition outdated external perceptions of the city with the new reality of the place.

On a smaller scale cities across the country are revitalizing their downtowns as cultural, sporting and entertainment districts, and in the process are redefining the way that people think about them. The downtown redevelopment projects in communities such as Brattleboro VT, Ann Arbor MI, Redwood City CA and Enumclaw WA have been initiated with the overall brand identity and city image in mind. They are not only aiming to attract more visitors, but to revitalize the interest of residents in the entertainment and recreational value of their own community.

One of the most dramatic examples of an entire city reinventing itself is Leavenworth WA. In 1962 community leaders were looking for ways to save the town during the demise of its timber industry. It had to redefine itself in order to prosper again. In collaboration with the Washington University Bureau of Community Development, city leaders developed the idea of using the town's beautiful natural surroundings as the backdrop to introduce a Bavarian theme. Instrumental in this effort were Pauline and Owen Watson, longtime residents who owned and operated Alpine Electric on Front Street.

In 1965 the decision was made by key business owners to adopt the Bavarian theme and commence remodelling their buildings. Pauline created sketches of some of the storefronts and presented these ideas to other business owners. An agreement was reached and Project Alpine was underway to guide the "Bavarianization" of Leavenworth, with Pauline serving as chairperson for the next ten years. One of the most impressive facts about this project is that it was financed with no federal assistance at all, simply dedicated people mortgaging everything they had! The town underwent an amazing transformation. The first six buildings were remodeled in 1965 and 1966, and the others soon followed. Today "Bavarian" Leavenworth is one of the most popular destinations in the state.[10]

While Leavenworth has successfully redefined itself, it is not an example that pleases everybody. Some cite it as lacking authenticity, being too contrived, and even turning the city into a theme park. This highlights the importance of community consultation to ensure that ideas for redevelopment are closely aligned with the community's vision and values. In the case of Leavenworth, it seems to have been a formula that has worked for both residents and its target audiences.

Reinventing a destination may take a totally different form when several nearby locations decide to redefine the way in which they position and present themselves. Interesting recent examples of this can be seen among regional communities that surround some major cities. This allows smaller DMOs to more efficiently and effectively deploy their marketing resources and harness the opportunities arising from their close proximity to much stronger destinations. Cleveland+ (www.ClevelandPlus.com), OneKC (www.ThinkOneKC) and Chicagoland (www.ChicagolandTravel.com) provide the marketing umbrellas for dozens of communities to develop sub-brands for Cleveland, Kansas City and Chicago in efforts to leverage their marketing investments.

## CHAPTER FOUR

# Prepare to Start: Mobilize the Forces

Like an athlete preparing to compete in a major event, you must complete a lot of careful and detailed preparation before getting to the starting line. Let's look at some of the preliminary actions needed to prepare a sound foundation to generate the support, understanding and endorsement of the branding project.

## It Must Be the CEO's Baby

The president or executive director of the DMO must be actively engaged in every aspect of the brand's development and breathe vitality into the assignment. We have found that the only way for the brand to take off is when the CEO "gets it" and has the passion, energy, skills and vision to make it work. If he or she takes a passive role, the brand will almost certainly fail.

Understandably, there may be many legitimate distractions that consume the CEO's time. However, the brand is at the heart of what will influence every activity that the destination will be involved in for years to come and thus worth every minute that he or she can devote to it. While the CEO may want to delegate aspects of the day-to-day management of the process to the marketing manager, he must remain intimately involved in crafting the brand strategy. This visible engagement by the CEO will ensure that he or she:

- Makes a strong statement to everyone that *this is important.*
- Strengthens their personal relationship, and that of the DMO, with key constituents.

- Fully understands and takes an active role in shaping the strategic rationale of the brand.
- Can present the brand with authority and enthusiasm.
- Ensures that the brand thrives in all areas of the organization and at all critical points of contact with customers.
- Leads the educative role in furthering the understanding of the brand.

## Take the Lead

One of the unexpected benefits of the collaborative approach is that it provides an unprecedented opportunity for the CVB or Chamber to showcase its role as a community and industry leader. Time and again, we have seen the process become the rallying point to re-energize the DMO, its constituents and the marketing of the city. The challenge is to sustain this heightened enthusiasm and use it as a catalyst to consolidate the DMO's position as one of the city's most valuable organizations. It is an ideal time to move people beyond turf building, internal politics and the dated opinions that may have prevailed in the past. DMOs rarely have a better chance to display their value to the community than through this process.

**We have noticed that the process tends to gain added credibility and support when the DMO reaches outside of "the usual suspects" to canvas the views of a wider range of constituents.**

We have noticed that the brand planning process tends to add credibility and support when the DMO reaches beyond "the usual suspects" to canvas the views of a wider range of constituents.

The Greater Tacoma Convention & Visitors Bureau strongly supports the consultative route. The bureau's Executive Director, Ruthie Rienert said, "The consultative planning process that we used generated incredible buy-in among our Board members, partners and stakeholders. It established the CVB as a community leader and contributed directly toward a better understanding and working relationship. We were able to make changes that probably would not have been possible for years had we not used external assistance and developed a strategy that had been built on collaboration and engagement."

## Great Leaders Lead to Great Brands

Cities are dynamic with myriad agendas, visions, objectives and egos – all in play at the same time. Most cities have multiple centers of influence and while many individuals and organizations are very customer, business, and future-oriented, others may be firmly locked in the past or may not want to see any changes. Others are less concerned about economic benefits as they are about the social and environmental impacts that marketing the community may bring. Still others question why money is being spent on branding and marketing when there are potholes in the streets. Communicating the benefits of branding to local citizens and organizations will help in winning support and boosting community pride.

Great brands are more likely to emerge when leaders step out of their comfort zone and show creativity, vision and courage. Their lead can be a powerful signal to everyone involved and may stimulate 'out of the box' ideas and collaboration among some of the most unlikely of partners. Brands are most likely to reach their greatest potential where there is passion, courage, and a strong commitment by the leadership of the city. While local opinions are very important, it is vital for leaders to understand that their external customers are the final arbiters on what will define the city's most potent brand.

The marketing and branding of cities can be complex and controversial. To avoid or minimize controversy, political and opinion leaders should be encouraged to understand the assignment and embrace the many benefits that the strategy will bring. When they fully grasp and support it, they are not only able to deflect criticism but will also become influential champions and open doors to signal that this project is important to constituents and the future of the city.

At times, achieving the brand vision and delivering the city's brand promise requires a leader to break from the status quo and exert the influence of his or her office. They may need to support a call for new resources, new organizational structures, a review of some city ordinances, beautification programs, and performance reviews. They may even be called on to slaughter a few "sacred cows" along the way. As I said earlier, in many respects branding is also an exercise in change management and relies very much on healthy relationships, cooperation and a genuine preparedness to adapt to new situations.

Another obstacle to branding cities has to do with turnover in leadership, especially those in cities and counties with term limits for elected officials. "Often, you'll have political leaders who agree that someone should put the place on the map but then say, 'It's not my job' because they will be out of here in a few years," says Rod Underhill. "There needs to be sufficient conviction among the other civic organizations and leaders that branding can withstand a turnover in leadership, and avoid stop-start marketing," he adds.[11]

**While local opinions are very important, it is vital for leaders to understand that their external customers are the final arbiters on what will define the most potent brand.**

It may take time, but before the project starts you need to invest the time to encourage the endorsement and participation of the leading executives, opinion leaders, and public officials who are likely to be instrumental in the long-term health of the brand. Some of these people may not be directly involved in the ongoing brand management, but their decisions and support may have profound leverage and influence. They should be exposed to the basic concept of branding and its benefits, and that it is more than an advertising campaign, new logo or slogan. Simply completing the brand strategy, and then presenting it to them is likely to result in a very weak brand or, even worse, controversy.

Brand planning must be based on open exchanges and collaboration to capture the information and insights needed to reveal the strongest brand identity possible. This may call for leaders and managers to break down territorial silos that may exist between, and within key organizations. This helps to ensure that there is no gap between what the city promises and the actual experiences that customers can enjoy.

This holistic or 360° approach to branding may require a break from the age-old way of doing things. Hence, opinion leaders need to be the catalysts and champions for a cultural shift at important points around the city. They also need to be onboard to assist in correcting any misunderstandings about the project and provide their unambiguous and hearty public endorsement.

It pays to be prepared for a variety of responses from individual leaders and organizations. To address their particular perspectives, different approaches and presentations may be necessary for discussions with the Board, community and business leaders, and potential brand partners. Carefully plan for each meeting by considering the benefits, agenda, and perspective relative to each.

## Give Them a Voice, Then Listen!

Canvassing the opinions of local constituents not only brings forward great ideas and perspectives, but can also provide important clues as to where the "land mines" or likely trouble spots may be later in the process. Importantly, consultation is extremely valuable in clearing the way to reveal the brand.

Within the community there will be residents, business, political and opinion leaders who will have comments, knowledge, and perspectives that should be considered. After they are identified, the level and nature of their involvement can be determined.

Brad Dean, President and CEO of Myrtle Beach Area Chamber of Commerce has some excellent advice for those starting a brand planning process for their city. Brad says, "One nugget of advice that I wish someone had offered me is this: 'The brand effort does not belong behind closed doors, in an ivory tower or within the boardroom. Involve everyone – the stakeholders, the Web programmer, the mayor, the media – involve anyone and everyone who has a reason to care. Involve your mother-in-law if you have to. Just make certain that anyone who has a vested interest gets a chance to be involved.' We didn't do this and, lo and behold, we rolled out the new brand to a chorus of boos and jeers. A few of our county council immediately announced they hated the idea, and the media blasted us. All of this could have been avoided if we had involved some of the key people in advance."

The task of pulling everyone together in a community with diverse political, cultural and social interests as those found in Santa Monica CA would seem like an impossible task. But, according to Misti Kerns, President and CEO of the Santa Monica Convention & Visitors Bureau, "When you can bring together 11 different interest groups, from the right and the left, and have everyone agreeing on a single item, then I'd have to say that's success, and that's what our branding experience has done for our community."[12]

Creating opportunities to participate can range from membership in the Brand Advisory Group, face-to-face interviews, attendance at a workshop, an invitation to complete a survey or periodic briefings about the progress. Don't sidestep the opportunity to invite critics and even those who may be cynical about such projects. By engaging them, their opinions may be changed, and even if they don't participate they may have greater respect for your efforts and provide support in other ways.

Over time, some community critics and cynics have been something of a source of amusement to us. From time to time, we have been warned about "Fred" because he is a "dreadful critic and always negative" about the Bureau or Chamber. Frequently, we find that when "Fred" is interviewed one-on-one, he finishes by being very supportive of the process and goals. Perhaps by speaking to an outsider, he can be less rebellious and save face by agreeing with us but not with other locals. In these cases, an outside firm is often a valuable surrogate who can act as a bridge to bring "Fred" to a point where he can make a positive contribution. The lesson is that it's far better to involve critics where they can express their opinions, be exposed to the brand benefits, and importantly, not disrupt the process or other participants. Even though it may not always be possible to convert critics into advocates for the project, you should at least aim to encourage the naysayers to become neutral and non-critical, rather than remaining negative and potentially undermine the project.

The number of potential participants in the process can be extensive, however we suggest that the following should be considered for inclusion:

- Association executives
- Businesses
- Chamber and CVB members
- Community leaders
- Developers and investors
- DMO's marketing vendors
- DMO staff
- Front line tourism employees
- Government
- Local media
- Lodging and hospitality executives
- Not-for-profit groups
- Opinion leaders
- Political leaders
- Religious leaders
- Sports representatives
- Visitor attractions and services
- Volunteers in visitor centers

## It Takes Objectivity and the Right Outside Expertise

One of the greatest challenges for those involved in the community's branding process is being objective and customer-focused. This may be the place where participants were born, educated, and now live. Hence, their bias may limit their view of the places from the perspective of an outsider. This highlights the need for outside advice to lend the impartiality and objectivity that is very difficult to get from within the community, DMO or city government. Many of our branding assignments are for communities that initially attempted to develop the strategy themselves. They found than an on outsider can succeed where stagnation and disagreement may otherwise limit progress because of entrenched attitudes and a reluctance to agree with long-standing opponents.

Engaging outside specialists also allows the community to harness the experience and skills that they may not have in a small city. The outside agency or consultant can guide the group through all of the difficult analysis and decisions that may be overlooked or glossed over by locals. Many cities have an increasing appreciation for the depth of experience and expertise that is needed to address the complexities and demands of destination branding. Destination Marketing Association International (DMAI) highlights this in their excellent publication, *Destination BrandScience* by Duane Knapp and Gary Sherwin, which states:

"Qualified, skilled brand expertise in strategic development is not easy to come by and even harder to identify. Typical RFPs use the words 'agencies'. While agencies may provide some of the services required for developing a strategy for destination brands, it may be a conflict of interest for the company currently doing the advertising or promotional campaign to do the assessment and create the promise.

Many advertising agencies or graphic design firms believe that they are in the business of brand development, and indeed some are. However, the real question to ask is: What is the vendor selling – advertising, graphic design or strategy? Ask yourself, if you were developing an RFP for a large bridge project, would you solicit construction firms to do the engineering? Of course not. You want the expertise of an independent expert to design the critical elements for success. True brand strategy requires the same high level of expertise."[13]

Al and Laura Ries, authors of "The 22 Immutable Laws of Branding," also bring into focus the importance of not allowing the brand strategy to be distracted by the tactical marketing programs. They state, "If you can build a powerful brand, you will have a powerful marketing program. If you can't, then all the advertising, fancy packaging, sales promotion and public relations in the world won't help you achieve your objective."[14]

## Select Your Brand Advisory Group

A Brand Advisory Group, representing a cross section of community and business organizations, should be assembled to oversee the brand planning process. Their main responsibility is to recommend approval and adoption of the brand strategy. Members should be carefully selected and only be appointed after a list of prospective candidates has been thoroughly evaluated. The group should ideally comprise 8-12 representatives, although there is no "correct" number. However, the more people in the group, the higher the risk that too many unrelated issues may start to play a role. This can slow things down, impair the sense of cooperation and objectivity that is needed, and dilute the brand itself.

The Pittsburgh Region Branding Initiative was the group responsible for overseeing the development of a brand strategy for Pittsburgh in 2002. I was surprised to see that it had 120 representatives on its Image Gap Committee – yes, 120! We can only wonder where they all sat at their meetings, let alone consider how each participant could make a truly meaningful contribution.

It is not unusual for Advisory Group members to develop a strong sense of ownership and pride in their contribution as the brand is defined. Their enthusiasm and commitment is priceless as the project moves forward.

**(Participants) may also realize that the DMO cannot achieve its objective alone and they all need to work in an active partnership. And most of all, they realize it's their "baby"!**

Many of them will eventually step forward to become active champions for the brand because they are so engaged and knowledgeable about all aspects of its creation. Hopefully, they will also come to see that the DMO cannot achieve its objectives alone and they all need to work in an active partnership. And most of all, they realize it's their "baby"!

In the mix of backgrounds and experience that will be represented on the Brand Advisory Group, it's helpful to invite some who are marketing and brand savvy, others who have a good pulse of the community, another who is politically savvy (and connected), and others who have a perspective of the community relationships with the outside world. This mix can lead to a broad spectrum of ideas, the constructive evaluation of concepts, and ensures that the approach is sensitive to the values and realities of the community.

At least one of the individuals participating in the meetings should be responsible for the eventual implementation and management of the brand. This helps keep things grounded and builds knowledge about the brand – and fosters a greater sense of ownership. We have found that the best Advisory Group participants are those who are:

- Objective and participate with an open mind
- Looking beyond their own self interest
- Passionate about getting the best possible result for the city
- Future-focused and not just looking at the short-term and tactical
- Well-respected and able to generate acceptance and support when the brand is launched
- Open to fresh ideas and eager to think "outside of the box"
- Aware that they have a stake in the success of the new brand, even if it is not directly focused on their organization
- Able to view the community from the customer's outside perspective

The Advisory Group's involvement should be woven throughout the brand planning process, especially at critical milestones. They may not necessarily be authorized to give approval or make major decisions, but they are an invaluable sounding board to provide guidance to the brand specialist and DMO executives. They should be representative of the community and, as a group, recommend approval of the final brand strategy to the client agency's board. This will ensure that solutions do not lose touch with market situations, resources, implementation capabilities, politics, and the self-image and values of the city.

The Group's involvement should start with an intensive briefing and discussion on branding, the planning process that will be followed, their role, and a discussion of their aspirations for the project. While some participants may be very experienced in marketing and branding, it still pays to provide this briefing. Starting with an informative presentation about branding cities ensures that everyone is on the same page.

Durham CVB President, Reyn Bowman sums it up well, "It's impossible to fathom just how much people misunderstand marketing in general and branding in specific. You can't emphasize enough what a brand is, and more important, what a brand isn't. Many people can't seem to grasp much beyond a logo or ad campaign. Advancing the thinking of stakeholders in regard to these subjects needs to be part of all community brand planning programs."

## Who Is Your Brand Steward?

A sustainable and strong brand is unlikely to grow in an ad hoc manner. It takes many guiding hands. After being launched, your brand will still need firm, consistent hands to meticulously follow the strategy and encourage players to perform their roles.

In addition to the DMO managing the brand, it requires someone within the organization to nurture, promote, manage, and "police" the brand as it is bought to life across all platforms and partners. This person is the most important friend that the brand will have. He or she is the brand steward and should be involved in the project from its earliest days. We tend to regard the brand steward as the person who is the main custodian of the brand, while the brand champions may be in various key organizations throughout the city and charged with advancing the brand vision for tourism, economic development, education, and so on. Brand champions are well respected individuals who are able to "open doors" and rally support for the brand within the community and key markets.

The brand steward must not only lead the efforts inside of the DMO, but also energize the outreach programs and briefings for members, marketing service vendors, and local partners. The steward is the enabler and protector who is responsible for activating the resources, talent, creativity, focus, and consistency to manage and grow this extremely valuable asset. He or she is responsible for maintaining the integrity of the brand by ensuring that all copy, images, design, messages and experiences conform to the brand objectives and the Destination Promise™.

The brand steward should be a strong communicator, and a marketing-savvy leader with the credibility, experience and vision to successfully guide the brand's implementation, use and delivery. It is common in a small city for the brand steward to be the CEO of the DMO. This person, while having ultimate responsibility, may work in close collaboration with the marketing manager and possibly a brand management committee to oversee the brand. These responsibilities should be reflected in their job descriptions and have the endorsement of the board to ensure that they are codified within the organization.

It is important to keep in mind that the brand doesn't belong to any one individual. It is the property of the entire community and its customers. In addition to reviewing internal uses, the brand steward must monitor the many forms of communications and experiences that emanate from the city's other messengers to encourage brand alignment, consistency and coherence across all applications.

## Match Your Goals and Budget

Whether your goal is to attract more visitors, new businesses or students, or to address an unfocused image, you must define your goals and objectives from the outset. Additionally, be sure that you have allocated sufficient funds to facilitate the most thorough brand planning process possible. These funds should be sufficient to engage a branding specialist to lead the process. When requesting the budget, you should also try to secure the resources for the launch and initial implementation of the strategy. This one-off allocation will prove to be a great investment because the brand can then be launched with the greatest impact possible, and without delay.

# CHAPTER FIVE

# The Seven Steps to a
# Community Brand

It is remarkable how many places rush to define their new brand following one or two brainstorming sessions that may have involved only their advertising agency and the DMO's staff. Equally as dangerous is when the agency presents a brand strategy comprising only a new logo and tagline to the DMO and stakeholders. Sometimes the approach is to first design the brand elements, then sell them to constituents. Efforts like these usually run out of steam very quickly or fail to ignite enthusiasm among stakeholders. When launched, more often than not, they don't have the support of key stakeholders because they were not treated as valued partners from the start. Sometimes it is not only a matter of what you do, but how you go about doing it. Dozens of community branding assignments have left me with no doubt that the collaborative and consultative approach leads to a much more accepted and sustainable brand.

In Durham, Reyn Bowman encouraged broad community buy-in when conducting Durham's brand planning. He said, "Durham is an incredibly complex place. We initiated a process of one-on-one interviews, balanced focus group discussions, opinion research and a representative Brand Advisory Board to ensure as much buy-in as possible. Additionally, once the brand was launched, we communicated periodic updates to hundreds of civic and business leaders and made presentations to local boards, civic clubs and organizations to help bring the brand to life and show people how to immediately incorporate it into their messages and operations."

Formulating a new brand is likely to take anywhere from five to more than twelve months, depending upon the size of the community, extent of the research, level of consultation, the decision-making process and the speed of decisions and approvals along the way.

## The 7A Destination Branding Process

The 7A Destination Branding Process recognizes the special nature of community-based branding. It encourages an approach that harnesses stakeholder buy-in from the start. Years of community branding assignments have shown us that this is essential to generate understanding and enthusiasm for the new brand. Importantly, it reinforces the need to build the brand from the inside out and ensures that brand planners are exposed to the heart and soul of the community.

**Figure 1: The 7A Destination Branding Process**

The steps in the *7A Branding Process* and the critical questions that must be answered are:

1. **Assessment and Audit**   What is the brand's place in the world?

2. **Analysis and Advantage**   What will the city be known for?

3. **Alignment**   What are the brand's relationships?

4. **Articulate**   How can the brand be expressed visually and verbally?

5. **Activation**   How will the brand come to life?

6. **Adoption and Attitudes**   How can stakeholders support the brand?

7. **Action and Afterward**   How will the brand be kept fresh and relevant?

The rigor and speed with which you are able to complete all steps will be influenced by the size of your community, its stage of development, scope of the brand, politics, available budget, time, and the authority and autonomy with which the DMO has been empowered to make decisions.

Communities that have followed this path find it energizing, educational, and a great unifying force. Most experience unexpected bonuses such as renewed support, revitalized relationships, and a rekindled sense of community purpose. It also serves to establish the DMO as an important leader in the community and as a future-focused organization.

As you proceed through each step, you will find that it is likely to be an iterative route and that things may not necessarily proceed in a smooth, linear fashion. At times you may be engaged in more than one step at a time. You may need to return to an earlier stage because the findings and solutions that have been revealed at a later stage. This also strengthens the brand because maintaining flexibility and openness contributes to a much stronger and healthier result.

## CHAPTER SIX

# Step One: Assessment –
# What's Your Place in the World?

We regard this first step as the most important and often the longest phase because it involves thoroughly reviewing and analyzing the world in which the new brand must excel. It establishes the knowledge base and foundation for everything that follows.

How you approach this step depends very much upon the size of the destination, its dynamics, past marketing efforts, and the available budget. Your actions will also be influenced by the relevance, quantity and quality of reports, past research, strategies, and publications that are available on the city. How readily the community becomes engaged in activities like this will also influence the approach that you take. These steps should uncover the current status of the city's marketing and image, where it came from, and the position that it needs to occupy in the future.

There are four fundamental questions that the city needs to answer:

- Who do we think we are?
- Who do our customers think we are?
- Who do we want to become?
- Who are we most likely to become?

During this phase you will be taking 'snapshots' to gain a picture of the current scene. It is vital to be objective and free from bias as you sift through this valuable information. It is not necessary to be judgmental or analytical at this point. Avoid jumping to premature conclusions, taking shortcuts, or falling in love with early ideas as this may compromise your thinking and creativity. Maintaining an open mind will enable you to capture a more accurate picture of where the brand is today, and where it can possibly go in future. Information overload may set in quickly as you sift through material from many sources including the disparate attitudes, values, beliefs, opinions, emotions, needs, and arguments that you may hear – sometimes all within one meeting!

While it may be tempting, don't bypass or minimize the importance of this step. To set your foot in the wrong place at this early stage may cause you to be miles off course when you start designing the rest of the brand identity. Keep an open mind, look for unexpected gems, and don't allow local politics and parochialism to overshadow the preferences and needs of external customers. At times there may be temptations and pressure to go faster or to skip some steps. Just as a great chef will not sacrifice speed for quality, you must adopt the same philosophy.

Revealing the brand relies on objective research, analysis, and a lot of creative thinking and collaboration. Michelangelo, one of the greatest sculptors of all time, described his skill as the ability to remove marble, chip by chip, to reveal the shape that was already residing within the stone. You could consider your brand as also encased in "stone" in the form of features, attitudes, thoughts, benefits, personality, perceptions, experiences, and a lot of irrelevant pieces. To find the masterpiece inside, you must "chip away" at all of the information, issues, distractions and components until you expose the distinctive brand essence within.

## Research: How to Obtain Answers to Your Questions

It is surprising how many places are flying blind when it comes to having a thorough knowledge of their customers and their marketing environment. One of the greatest hurdles, particularly for small cities, is the lack of actionable research to support their decision-making.

Therefore, marketing decisions are often based totally on "conventional wisdom" that later proves to be unreliable. It is impossible to know what customers think and feel without some form of research. Simply put, the more committed that cities can be to their research efforts, the better prepared they are to make informed and objective decisions.

Research may appear to be too expensive, or even a waste of money. No doubt, you can certainly invest a lot in research and still end up making poor decisions. But research doesn't have to be a complex, expensive, or wasteful exercise. Consider it as a systematic way to gather needed facts and information. Even when we apply this simple definition, many destinations still struggle because they don't have even a basic information gathering system in place.

We agree that it's a challenge for small destinations to budget for sophisticated research projects, but it shouldn't mean that they abandon all efforts. It is still possible to employ a range of cost effective research techniques. While they may not be as comprehensive or as robust as some of those conducted by a specialist research agency, they are certainly better than flying blind. Some of the ways in which research can be used to inform your brand development decisions include:

- Assessing the status of the current brand

- Identifying priority markets, customer demographics and behavioral characteristics

- Gauging perceptions and attitudes toward the place

- Assessing competitors

- Identifying and testing the city's ideal positioning

- Assessing customer satisfaction

- Selecting and testing taglines and logos

- Monitoring brand performance

A basic research program can provide a wealth of valuable

information that will result in a much stronger brand than simply going on gut instinct and a few opinions. The smaller your marketing budget, the smaller your margin for error, and the more imperative it is for you to make absolutely certain that you are spending your available budget on the right markets and customers, and employing the right messages.

Brad Dean, President and CEO of Myrtle Beach Area Chamber of Commerce spells out the value of research, "Through our branding process we learned a lot about what our customers did, and did not like. There is a great tendency to want to nudge the consumer's views aside and exert your will over the process, but the integrity of the brand is immediately compromised when that takes place. Rather, by removing ourselves from the testing process and simply evaluating the results, we were able to clearly define the brand and push implementation almost immediately."

No matter the size of your budget, it comes down to asking the right questions of the right people, under the right conditions. Broadly, your options can be divided into two forms of research collection: primary and secondary.

## Primary Research

Primary research refers to the information that you originate yourself. This research may be conducted by you or by engaging a research agency.

Knowing what current and prospective customers think is vitally important to branding assignments because it enables you to better understand their needs and more comprehensively evaluate your positioning options. Gauging perceptions through consumer surveys enables you to compare and evaluate the city on criteria and attributes that are important to the customer. While comprehensive studies may be outside of the available budget of many small cities and regions, there are a number of cost-effective survey options available. Methods of consulting stakeholders include:

### Face-to-Face Interviews

Interviews with local constituents and external partners such as meeting planners and tour operators are an invaluable source of insights, opinions and information. Frequently you can obtain information from these interviews that is not possible to obtain from focus groups and workshops. It is sometimes better to engage certain individuals through face-to-face interviews because they may be reluctant to express their true thoughts and feelings in a public setting. This particularly applies to political and business leaders, or critics of the DMO or City. Interviews can also be conducted with current and prospective customers via telephone, email, or in person.

### Focus Groups and Workshops

These group meetings can be conducted in the city, as well as in source markets, and usually comprise eight to fifteen participants. Rather than forming each gathering from the same interest groups, e.g. lodging or attractions, try to sprinkle them with participants with diverse points of view. Focus groups are valuable for exploring reactions and attitudes toward possible ideas and solutions. They can discuss general attitudes toward the city, positioning options, potential brand platform elements, and provide input in regard to brand experience issues.

### Community Forums

One of the benefits of this forum is providing a large number of interested people the opportunity to directly participate in the process. Depending upon the community, the number of participants may range from thirty to more than

a hundred. The downside of a community forum is that the large number of participants can be a deterrent for some wanting to express their true feelings, or may be dominated by a few outspoken individuals. A skilled facilitator can mitigate these issues.

### Community Survey

Those who cannot participate in interviews, workshops, or community forums, may be able to provide their input in the form of a survey. Affordable online options such as Surveymonkey.com and Zoomerang.com provide powerful Internet-based survey and analytical tools that are ideal for community surveys.

### Secondary Research

Sometimes called desk research, secondary research generally involves the review and analysis of published information, data and reports that are readily available. This is less costly than primary research, but may not provide the customized information that is accessible through primary research.

Valuable secondary information can be obtained by reviewing:

- Trends and transactions relating to lodging, tourism,

relocation, and economic development for the city, region, and state.

- All tourism, cultural, economic development, and other relevant research for the city, region, and state that has been completed in recent years.

- Past marketing, collateral materials, Websites and

third party promotion of the city, e.g. State and regional tourism offices, commercial guidebooks, tour operator brochures, and material from the local tourism industry.

- Local and target market media archives to assess their coverage of the city, customer groups, and competitors.

## Take A 360° View

During the Assessment phase, the idea is to take an unbiased 360-degree view that includes an understanding of internal and external customers, their needs, competitor capabilities, and uncovering distinctive strengths, trends, customer experiences, attitudes, personality and the capabilities of the city.

An honest self-examination is essential and requires an objective appraisal of not only the strengths, but also areas where the city experience may be considered deficient or weak. This may be difficult for some locals to admit, particularly those closely associated with the subject or issue. Without this honesty, the brand may be considerably weakened and short-lived. Among the perspectives that should be evaluated are:

1. Internal stakeholders
2. Strengths and assets
3. Performance
4. Communications and marketing audit
5. External stakeholders
6. Competitors

7. Customers
8. Experiences
9. Trends

## 1. Internal Stakeholders: What Is Their Perspective?

Those communities that are most successful in their branding efforts have usually taken the time to engage residents, as well as business, community and opinion leaders. As difficult as it may sound, these sometimes competing and contradictory voices need the opportunity to make a contribution. Interestingly, we have found that the smaller the community, the more acute the need for a collaborative and inclusive approach. While it is important to listen to local voices, never lose sight of the most important voice of all – the customer's.

## 2. Strengths and Assets: What Makes Us Different?

At the heart of a brand are the strengths or competitive advantages that set it apart and make it different from others. These include both physical and intangible attributes. They can be identified through first-hand evaluation of the place through onsite visits, content analysis of marketing materials, and your customer and stakeholder research. Some of the strongest assets may be obscured or not readily apparent. It is important to recognize that even though you have outstanding natural beauty, fantastic architecture, superb wineries, or other physical attributes, it is how the place makes customers feel that will ultimately determine your reputation and value. George Whitfield, a UK-based destination branding expert, put it best when he said, "The most beautiful landscape in the world will not compensate for an inability to make a visitor or guest feel wanted, welcome and delighted. Branding is all about making an experience of a place as memorable, different, and exceptional as it can possibly be."[15]

An onsite assessment should involve experiencing the community through the senses of a customer. Take time to walk the streets, drive around, visit restaurants, check out attractions, use public facilities, phone offices and test services. How the city looks and functions is critical to the appeal and sustainability of its brand. The appearance of the city sends a strong message to visitors as they walk or drive through its streets. What are the messages that your city is sending? What are its sight, sound, smell, touch, and taste encounters?

**Nothing can "kill" a place with inferior visitor experiences faster than effective promotion.**

If you have ever been attracted to a place by its advertising, and have then experienced vague reservations agents, untidy streets, inferior accommodations, indifferent retailers, poor signage, and uninteresting museum exhibits, then you know that there are more important priorities for places like this than an advertising campaign to attract more visitors. Places like this are leaking income, jobs and taxes – not to mention their brand equity and reputation. Nothing can "kill" a place with inferior visitor experiences faster than effective promotion. The more people are attracted to a place like this and then exposed to its inadequacies, the faster and wider the negative word of mouth will spread, thus precipitating a rapid downward spiral.

The search for the city's brand strengths starts by examining:

- *The People*: How they influence the city is often at the heart of the brand. Their values, heritage, traditions and culture are likely to inspire the features of the place and may be directly reflected its personality.

- *The Physical Attributes*: These comprise the setting, climate, architecture, streets, industries, transport, museums, restaurants, produce, attractions, facilities, and events.

- *The Tangible Benefits*: These incorporate elements such as its access, costs, service, safety and cleanliness, transactions, education system, interpretation and whether it has a business-friendly nature.

- *The Intangibles*: These may include its ambience, atmosphere, experiences, community pride, personality, flavor, authenticity, image, reputation, sensory stimulation and trust.

## 3. Performance: What Has Been Achieved?

Reviewing a wide variety of metrics will provide insights into the strengths, weaknesses and opportunities facing the city. Some of the questions that you should consider include:

- How has the city performed over the past decade?
- Has it performed the same, worse or better than competitors?
- Have new industries, businesses or opportunities emerged or declined?
- How has the visitor economy performed?
- How have the lodging and retail sectors performed?
- Are there surveys that monitor customer opinions, attitudes and satisfaction?

After examining available tourism data, you should be able to uncover issues relating to seasonality, source markets, market share, length of stay, yield, and dispersal throughout the community that require attention.

## 4. Communications and Marketing Audit: What Do They Reveal?

A communications audit provides an understanding of the focus, creativity, content, and effectiveness of current and past communications produced by the city's leading messengers. It should also demonstrate the level of consistency in the messages from the various entities.

Start by assembling past advertising, Websites, trade show displays, brochures, photo images, and media clippings to review their content, themes, design, and style. Don't forget about the marketing communications of key partners. Next, review the results of past marketing efforts, including analysis of traffic to the Website, advertising responses and conversion rates and inquiries from prospective customers as well as customer complaints. What worked? What didn't? Examine the content of articles and features on the city to identify themes, accuracy, and tone of the coverage.

The marketing communications that should be included in the audit are:

- Advertising
- Annual reports
- Bid documents
- Billboards
- Brochures
- Business cards
- Direct mail materials
- Email newsletters
- Image library
- Media clippings
- Meeting planning guide
- Newsletters
- Presentation folders
- Press kits and releases
- Sales kits
- Staff communications
- Stationery
- Street signs
- Tour planning guides
- Trade show displays
- Uniforms and costumes
- Videos and DVDs
- Wayfinding signs
- Websites

## 5. External Stakeholders: What Are They Thinking?

There are frequently important individuals and organizations outside the community who play a pivotal role in influencing perceptions of the city. They have a very deep understanding of the place with an objectivity and customer focus that local residents don't always have. They can more readily identify the blemishes, as well as the opportunities and strengths that can lead to improved performance.

Members of the city's distribution channels should be involved in the research process. It may seem somewhat strange to use the term 'distribution' because tourism and economic development products can't be stored and transported like food or consumer goods. However, distribution is the term used to describe the vital information, sales, and transaction links between a destination and its end-customers. This informal network of intermediaries enables a place to reach and influence more distant target audiences. They may involve packaging and promoting tourism products to the area, selling real estate, or providing advice on relocation options.

These external stakeholders may include:

- Association executives
- Booking services
- Business media
- Cruise operators
- Government departments
- Incentive travel planners
- Marketing service vendors
- Meeting and event planners
- Online travel companies
- Public officials
- Real estate agents
- Receptive tour operators
- Regional and national media
- Regional and state tourism organizations
- Site location specialists
- Tour operators
- Transportation operators
- Travel agents
- Visitor information centers

## 6. Competitors: How Do We Stack Up?

Knowing exactly who your competitors are can be more involved than it might appear. Many cities simply regard their competitors as the places that are in their immediate vicinity. This overlooks the underlying factors that may be motivating customers, and the myriad options they have.

Your competitors are very likely to change depending upon the specific market segments you're addressing. The reality is that it's your customers who determine who your competitors are. A good way to approach this dilemma is to consider: *Who wins the customers when we lose?* For instance, depending upon your market, competitors could be major events, a shopping center, a resort, or a National Park, in addition to neighboring cities. The answers may also change depending upon the time of year. For example, Stowe VT attracts snow sport enthusiasts during winter, as well as a wide variety of outdoor enthusiasts and sightseers during the other months. This will bring Stowe into competition with different places at different times of the year.

Possible sources of competitor intelligence include:

- The observations and experiences of your staff and partners.
- Analysis of their advertising, Websites and promotional material.
- First-hand experience as a visitor.
- Travel products such as packages, cruises, and tours.
- The marketing activities and products of the organizations in the competitor city.
- Websites that capture the comments of past visitors.
- Media coverage including trade publications.
- Statewide economic and tourism performance trends.
- Incentives for business relocation.

## 7. Customers: Who Are They?

The most important people in the entire process are your customers. The ultimate goal is to influence the way that they think, feel, and act in regard to your community. To achieve this you need a thorough understanding of who they are, their perceptions, and what really motivates them. You also need to determine whether the brand should be prepared for international, regional, state, or local markets.

Some destination marketers don't clearly define their markets and then make the mistake of trying to appeal to all markets and all people. The prospect of targeting all markets just isn't feasible because it's too expensive, risky and wasteful. Even though the Internet may get you part of the way there and you think your product is "just right" for everyone, in reality the city must be more targeted in its approach. You will have to segment the market and establish priorities – the right product at the right price and at the right time and place. The more fine tuned the audience and the more that the brand can be honed to address their specific needs, the better the return on your marketing dollars.

Some of the critical questions that customer research should answer are:

- Where do they live?
- Why do they visit or do business with you? How often? With whom?
- How do they feel about the city?
- What do they want from a destination like yours?
- What are the benefits they are seeking?
- Is the market large enough? Will it yield sufficient return?

## 8. Experiences: How Are We Doing at Critical Moments?

Quite simply a brand is a promise. To be even more precise it is the promise of an experience that must be kept, because the essential core of the brand is how it will make customers feel. This is why we advocate that destination branding requires a 360° focus to address the customer's total destination experience.

A corporate brand may have anywhere from five to fifty points where it is in touch with its customers. On the other hand, the number for a destination brand could be endless because there is no limit to the points at which customers can interact with it. Beyond the obvious hotels, restaurants, stores, information centers and airport, a destination can touch customers through the weather, the media, its citizens, as well as through friends and relatives, and even health providers and supermarkets. Many of the contact points are out of the direct control of the DMO. Others such as Websites, advertising, brochures and visitor service can be more easily influenced by the DMO and its partners.Unlike the manager of a corporate brand, the destination's brand manager must work with many organizations and individuals over whom he or she usually has no control or authority, let alone the ability to request conformity to the city's brand platform and guidelines. They must, however, try to influence their quality at the most critical moments of contact with visitors and customers.

Later in the process it will be necessary to revisit this experience audit to identify the actions needed at critical points of contact to ensure delivery of your Destination Promise™. Are there gaps? What are the causes of the gaps? What is the underlying cause of the problems?

## 9. Trends: Which Wave Will You Catch?

If you have ever been surfing, then you know that timing is everything. Catching a wave at the right moment can be the experience of a lifetime. On the other hand, bad timing can result in being dumped and surfacing with a mouth full of sand. Branding can be a lot like that, too! If you catch a trend moving in the wrong direction, it can be much the same as being dumped by a wave. Aligning with a strong trend, however can add charisma, celebrity and prosperity to your brand. Cultural and economic trends can have a profound influence on customer tastes and preferences. Are there economic, social, cultural and technical trends that are likely to help or hinder the acceptance and performance of your brand?

## Questions

Important questions to be answered during Step One are:

- What is it about the city that is distinctive, different or special that competitors cannot easily match?

- What is it like to be a customer of your community?

- What are the markets in which the city wants to compete?

- What is the structure of the city's markets and the distribution channels?

- What are the perceptions and attitudes toward your city?

- What is the effect when the economic development and tourism marketing materials are seen together?

- What is the vision for the community?

- What is the content, tone, and trend of media articles and coverage of the city?

- What were the results of past marketing efforts?

- Who are the main competitors? Who are secondary competitors?

- How does the competitor group change for each priority market?

## CHAPTER SEVEN

# Step Two: Analysis and Advantage – What Will You Be Known For?

Once you have all of the information and data collated from Step One, you can now thoroughly distill and analyze it. This will provide a realistic picture of the brand's dimensions and what may be needed to address any gaps and shortcomings. Most importantly, it sets the stage for you to claim your positioning and competitive advantage, and for defining the objectives and strategies needed to build the brand.

## Stake Your Claim

Positioning a community requires careful consideration of three dynamic elements. You should have already collated the information relevant to each. These are (1) the needs of target customers, (2) destination strengths (both tangible and intangible), and (3) competitor strengths. The recommended positioning should only be finalized after the values and opinions of stakeholders have been taken into account.

**Figure 2: Opportunity Modeling for Optimum Positioning**

Figure 2 illustrates the process of opportunity modeling in which filtering and refining the wealth of qualitative and quantitative information leads to defining the optimal positioning. The strongest positioning is at the intersection of these three concentric circles. This is where you can establish the most meaningful edge or competitive advantage that competitors can't easily match.

Your most powerful positioning should place the city outside of the "gravitational field" of your competitors, yet where it can resonate with greatest clarity and relevance for key customers. If it is not clearly differentiated or remains in the shadow of major competitors, the city will always be seen as a pale option, unless it demonstrates and proves how it is different, relevant and can add value. Competing head to head with more formidable competitors on the basis of the same positioning and value proposition is never a sustainable long-term strategy.

The following are some of the variables that are commonly used to position a destination. Frequently, it may take a combination of variables to claim the most distinctive and potent point of difference.

- Architecture and design
- Attractions
- Celebrity and fame
- Climate
- Cuisine and wine
- Culture
- Emotional benefits and feelings
- Ethnicity
- Events
- History
- Industry and local products
- Influence and power
- Landmarks and icons
- Legends and myths
- Location and access
- Natural environment
- Nightlife
- People
- Personality and values
- Physical attributes
- Social benefits
- Sport

## The Criteria for Power Positioning

During the opportunity modeling phase, each positioning option should be critically evaluated against the following three criteria.

## DIFFERENTIATION

Strong brands stand out from the crowd and are different in ways that matter to customers. How important is your point of difference? Is it valuable enough to allow you to charge a premium price? Will it allow you to lead with products and experiences that competitors can't easily match? Does the target audience see your city as the only or best choice based on this proposition?

## RELEVANCE

In order to be relevant the positioning must be more than just different. If the point of difference is not important enough to stimulate or peak customer's interest in the place, then it will not stimulate demand. Being the *Grass Seed Capital of the World* may mark Linn County OR as different, but is it relevant to external customers, particularly prospective visitors? Likewise, positioning based on friendliness or community pride may not be meaningful or relevant to external audiences. The positioning needs to be based on strengths that are valued and are meaningful and will have the strongest connection with key audiences and lead to increased respect and loyalty.

## TRUTHFUL

Sustainable marketing demands that the place be true to itself and not attempt to present itself as something it's not. Is the positioning credible, authentic and believable? Can you always deliver on this promise? For instance, is the community trying to position itself as a cultural city, but without an active or prosperous arts community or quality restaurants? Are other cities already seen as owning this positioning and attributes?

## Brand Positioning: Claiming the Most Valuable Real Estate

A city's most valuable real estate is usually not the largest buildings that form its skyline. Rather, it is the space in the hearts and minds of its customers where they store all of their thoughts, feelings, and perceptions about the place. This is the territory that influences where they will visit, work, live, shop, invest or study, and where you find the memories and feelings that build respect and give you preference over competitors. Your challenge is to stake your claim on the most valuable piece of this real estate. This is *positioning*, and represents how you want customers to think and feel about the place. It is how the city's key stakeholders want targeted customers to see it relative to other options.

Defining your community's brand position is, without a doubt, the most important and trickiest part of the entire destination branding process. While the logo and tagline frequently receive a lion's share of attention during the planning phases, it is actually the task of pinpointing the positioning that should be given the most consideration. If you don't get this part right, everything else will miss its mark, since it is the positioning that informs and shapes all other elements of the brand strategy – including the logo, tagline and marketing communications.

Positioning helps to refine the components of the brand platform and shapes the *Destination Promise*™. Doing it right means not rushing it – and it isn't for the faint of heart. The strongest positioning frequently involves temporarily sacrificing some attributes in order to select the most enticing, meaningful and differentiating. The objective is to secure the largest number of high yield customers possible, while upholding the community's values and achieving its strategic objectives.

In the hundreds of destination marketing plans that we have reviewed over the years, we find so many of them totally overlook positioning. Frequently, there is not a single sentence on the subject. One of the great advantages of a structured brand planning approach, such as our *7A Process*, is that it forces consideration of this pivotal building block. If you overlook this step, you will likely find yourself competing head to head with stronger competitors or constantly changing messages. Then, with a weaker position all that you may have to compete with is a lower price and a vague value proposition. And just because a place is different or even unique doesn't necessarily mean that target audiences will find it attractive.

For the customer, the right position gives them the optimum combination of attributes and benefits. As a marketer, positioning is important because it keeps the brand on the right course and should be a source of inspiration for your branding team and partners for years to come. Positioning involves examining the context and space in which the city fits into the customer's world. There is no shortcut or room for politics, parochialism, appeasement or self-interest. This is quite a challenge for communities that may have many competing voices, but it is essential that you avoid a watered down and meaningless positioning.

Another way to consider the role of positioning and branding is to think of positioning as what you want the city to be known for, and the role of the branding programs as being the means to secure

and reinforce it in the hearts and minds of customers. The best positioning is based on a single thought or idea. This is genuinely difficult for most cities to agree upon, because of the complex matrix of products, markets and stakeholders that it is trying to satisfy. Not to mention an overabundance of competitors.

## No, You Can't Have – or Be – It All!

The decision as to which components should lead the positioning can be controversial. Obviously, not all aspects are of equal interest and value to customers. For this reason, the city must lead with those that will best attract, motivate, and satisfy target audiences. Too often, the ideal point of distinction becomes blurred and diluted by a lack of consensus and the "We have everything," "It's all here," or "The center (or heart) of it all" syndrome.

The "we have everything" syndrome is one of the most common pitfalls in securing strong positioning. It has also been termed the 'air raid shelter' syndrome[16] because participants don't want to leave anything or anyone out. The result can be a ball of self-serving fluff with no meaningful or distinctive edge to help the place stand out. The idea may play well to local audiences and it may be seen as a good compromise because it is inclusive and seems to make everyone in the community happy (a dead giveaway you're on the wrong track!). But being inclusive and making locals feel good, without resonating positively with customers is the absolute antithesis of what good positioning and branding should be about.

Not even the largest places can be all things to all people. New York City realizes that it doesn't have resorts, ski slopes, natural wonders and wineries. Successful place brands are those that are able to clearly differentiate themselves, hit customer hot buttons, and simplify customer choices. Fundamental to achieving this is for city leaders and stakeholders to take an objective, customer-focused view and play their very strongest hand.

Recently, there has been a cavalcade of high priced brand strategies for communities with positioning that is so "warm and fuzzy" that I can only guess that they were chosen to keep the locals happy. These

are a waste of time and money. Someone was not asking the simple customer-focused questions, such as "what's in it for me?"

Whisper Brand Strategy Consultants presents a very strong critique of these warm and fuzzy or "adulatory messages" as they call them. They state that "Adulatory claims and *cheerleader messages* gain credibility among those on the inside responsible for the brand – executives, members of the Board, administration, brand managers, other organizational leaders. They feel great about cheerleader messaging because the message is so darn POSITIVE. But each of these insiders is already convinced – they are paid to pay attention – while the consumer they wish to influence is not. Instead, the consumer has to pay, literally, when they pay attention – they pay with their time and mental effort, neither of which consumers are likely to invest when a brand shouts in self-flattery ....which is why they are so numbingly unmemorable, and irrelevant."[17]

Strong and meaningful positioning often means a degree of sacrifice and sometimes hard or unpopular decisions.

The city must single-mindedly zero in on its one core truth, DNA or essence that will connect customers with the city's most compelling experiences. This may involve a combination or blend of a few attributes, characteristics or benefits to provide the originality or distinctiveness that will strike a chord.

### Intangibles Are Cool

No community is one-dimensional. It's always more than its physical attributes and features. It's cool, relaxed, laid-back demeanor and celebrity can be as attractive as its physical assets like the beach, jazz bars, outdoor restaurants, and galleries. It is often intangibles like culture, heritage, personality and atmosphere that have the most profound influence on defining what makes the place distinctive.

Suburban sprawl, cookie cutter developments, and big box retail outlets are creating an urban sameness which is challenging leaders to express the attractiveness, individuality and distinctiveness of their communities. Increasingly, they need to explore their intangible dimensions in order to distinguish themselves.

"Why the sudden interest in distinctiveness by cities? For a long time, cities yearned for Wal-Marts and McDonalds," one planning expert told the Seattle Times. "Now that we have them and see what they mean to our community landscapes, we're realizing we need something different. We want our authenticity to show itself."[18]

Others are recognizing that most of what cities offer is experiential, explaining why their product is mainly intangible. We don't actually purchase the street, harbor, or café. We experience them, rather than possess them. What is important and memorable is how they make us feel.

Sometimes, there may be gray areas in distinguishing between the physical and intangible attributes. For example price, distance, taste, size, and beauty could be considered as being either intangible or tangible. Perceptions may only exist in the customer's mind, but they are extremely powerful and the positive ones must be nurtured and protected. They serve to distinguish a place as being fun, exciting, romantic or some other feeling. To truly build a powerful brand, perceptions have to work in concert with the reality of the place in order to mold its reputation, credibility, and appeal.

### The Strength of an Intangible Umbrella

The greatest challenge in branding cities is gaining consensus for positioning with a singular focus. The positioning should be capable of encouraging the greatest number of stakeholders and partners to buy into it, and actively use it. By focusing on the strongest emotional benefits and intangibles, the ideal brand enables partners to reach and influence key markets. For example, rather than just promoting wineries, being known as a place for "good living" will also open opportunities for fine dining, quality entertainment, boutique stores, spas, resorts, and galleries. This creates a stronger and more satisfying proposition because it allows the city to claim a more distinctive positioning that appeals to more customers than if it had relied on the physical elements of wine and wineries alone.

Intangibles, particularly those with emotional or social benefits, provide stronger and more enticing rewards enabling destinations to form special bonds with their customers. They also create a more inclusive and flexible brand that embraces more local partners as opposed to positioning that is based solely on their physical attributes. For example, if Arlington TX had based its brand on its theme parks alone, it would have limited the list of local partners, who could relate directly to the brand. But, by basing its positioning on the emotional benefits of family fun and excitement, the city was able to offer a stronger and more meaningful set of experiences that also embrace Texas Rangers baseball, museums, and recreation. Their combined brand name/tagline *Fun Central* sums it up very well in a distinctive and evocative way. With some modification to their individual positioning, many local partners are now able to more easily align their operations and marketing with the overall brand than had it been based on the concept of theme parks alone.

Relying on tangible attributes alone allows competitors to more easily copy, weaken or match your claims of superiority. There won't be another

Grand Canyon, but features such as outdoor recreation and natural assets may be shared with other communities. Instead, strive to be associated with a lucrative, higher-level intangible benefit or feeling.

### Unique: To Be, or Not To Be?

Being unique simply means "the only one of its kind." Does that mean unique in the entire world? The overused term "unique" is so misused and worn-out, and above all, a status that is very difficult to achieve. Among the 20,000 incorporated cities in the USA, there are few that can claim to be truly unique on the basis of characteristics that are important to customers. Identifying the ideal positioning must be considered in the context of the audience that the community is trying to influence and within the set of competitors that the customer may consider. Regardless, some will insist that all cities are unique, like fingerprints or snowflakes, no two are exactly the same. While some consumer products or fast moving goods can claim a positioning that is truly unique, this is much harder for cities because they have many more competitors. Not only are so many of them physically alike, many of them even have the same names. For example, there are 150 Jacksons, 101 Lincolns, and 57 Springfields in the United States.

While major cities such as London, New York, Sydney, Hong Kong, and Rio de Janeiro battle within the global context, most small cities should be more narrowly focused on being distinctive and expressing their competitive advantage within their competitor set. This usually involves comparisons to places closer to home. Does it matter if there is a small city in Utah positioning itself as the place for enjoying the therapies and relaxation of herbal gardens, when there are places in Vermont and Florida doing the same? Probably not, because their target markets are within their immediate regions! It also depends upon the intangible benefits and emotional rewards that they are projecting. And of course, they should never have the same or similar tagline! If those similarly positioned destinations are not places that the Utah city's customers would realistically consider visiting as an alternative, then they are not direct competitors and the similarities may not matter.

## Leave Room to Grow

Because a city is dynamic and constantly evolving, its positioning should be aspirational – that is, it needs room to grow. This allows for trends and developments that may have a profound effect on the brand. The outstanding art glass of famed local artist Dale Chihuly was one of the inspirations for Tacoma WA to base its brand positioning on being a center for world-class art glass. Developed two years before the city opened two new major art museums, the CVB and the City had the opportunity to mobilize stakeholders and commence the local advocacy and marketing communications to reposition the place. Of course, in cases like this you must take care to ensure that the city does not make promises it can't keep, or claim a position that it isn't going to reach within a reasonable period of time. Tacoma successfully bridged this gap to reposition itself and is now amazing its visitors with the transformation that has taken place.

Similarly, Atlanta GA had the future in mind when determining their brand strategy in June 2007. Mayor Shirley Franklin said in launching the branding process, "In the next few years, Atlanta will see the opening of many exciting, world-class attractions, which is great news for visitors. Promoting our city and its hospitality and tourism industry is key to reaching those goals. Now is the right time to launch a brand campaign like this."

## There's Money in Hot Dogs and Beer

As I said earlier, some cities, or at least community leaders and marketers, find it difficult to agree on a single idea or concept on which to set the destination apart. Their main fear is that something or someone will be left out. I like to use a baseball analogy to illustrate this dilemma. In baseball it seems that the best batters and pitchers receive just about all of the pre-game publicity. Many of these guys make millions of dollars a year. There is another group who gets no pre-game publicity, but also make millions a year – the operators of the concession stands. The hot dogs and beer can be very enjoyable, but they are not going to motivate you to go to a game. However, it's just not baseball without them. They are integral to this all-American experience, yet you hear nothing of them until you go to the game. Both need each other. If the beer and hot dog sellers were the ones featured in the media and not the pitchers and batters, none of them would make as much income.

The lesson is that you lead with what is most relevant and enticing at the particular time when customers are making their decisions. Similarly, the message of a community must be very narrowly focused on its most compelling message to attract attention, and then follow with support attractions, services and experiences. Putting them in the wrong order would be no different to hoping to fill the baseball stadiums by featuring the hot dog and beer sellers on the sports pages.

### Parity Isn't a Winning Position

Wherever they go, visitors expect to find high quality lodging, good restaurants, well-designed public spaces, and friendly people. Avoid positioning that is based on entry-level attributes or points of parity that are simply expected of all places. If an attribute is a basic entry requirement, i.e. friendliness, good service, attractive prices or cleanliness, it is unlikely to represent a mean-

ingful differentiating factor that will deliver added value or sustainable positioning.

An exception to this rule is when the destination may present a unique angle and exert ownership over a particular entry-level attribute and it is sustainable within their competitive set. Australia, for example, was able to extend the meaning and value of friendliness through its highly successful and humorous advertising campaigns that invited Americans to "*Come and Say G'day*" and promising "*I'll slip an extra shrimp on the barbie for you.*" By using its friendliness and distinctive accent to full advantage, Australia was able to break through the media noise and clutter to connect with Americans by showing its unusual wildlife, natural wonders, and cosmopolitan cities in a humorous and engaging way. But individual Australian states and cities cannot position themselves using their friendliness in this way.

Similarly, "Southern hospitality', is an appeal for prospective travelers to the southern states of the USA. However, while the region may be able to use it as a differentiating factor, "Southern hospitality" can be tricky for individual cities to lead with because it is a characteristic expected of all places in the South.

While a destination may have defined its individual characteristics and decided to position them as distinctive, a more objective and honest assessment might reveal that they are also common to many nearby places. For example, in the Pacific Northwest many communities try to pin their positioning on their natural scenery, mountains, or a high quality of life. The reality is that nearly all communities in the Northwest are natural, beautiful, and enjoy a high quality of life. These qualities are almost the price of admission to play the community marketing game in this region. Those that want to base their positioning on their natural environment or quality of life had better have superiority in some other aspect of these experiences. "Pretty much everyone's got rivers and mountains in Washington," the mayor of Snoqualmie WA said. "The question is "How do you set yourself apart?"[19] The congestion in positioning options can also be seen where Anchorage AK and near neighbor The Yukon, Canada both covet

the "larger than life" positioning that is important to their adventure-seeking visitors. This crowded position is highlighted by the similarity of Anchorage's tagline *Big. Wild. Life* and The Yukon's *Larger than life.*

Similarly, cities in California and Florida have to provide much more than sunny weather, and cities in Arizona need more than easy access to high quality golf courses and desert scenery.

"We've worked to strengthen our brand marketing initiatives on what could be considered the somewhat 'gray' areas of location and service," says Maura Allen Gast, Executive Director of the Irving Texas Convention and Visitors Bureau. "By positioning Irving as 'In Between, Far Above,' we are differentiating our destination on the relevance and benefit of being 'in between' Dallas and Fort Worth, as well as providing outstanding guest service throughout the destination at a level 'far above' expectations." While 'location' and 'service' may be considered threshold requirements to be a successful destination, in the context of Irving's customer needs, competitive environment and challenging identity, this is appropriate."

## The Brand's Engine Room: The Brand Platform

The brand platform provides the foundation on which the Destination Promise™ and all future brand experiences will be based. It is the nucleus or engine of the brand. Here we outline what the place wants to become, what it believes in being, and what makes it distinctive. These elements have been crystallized from the interviews, workshops, research and the analysis and filtering conducted during the opportunity modeling phase.

The brand platform will influence brand behavior, shape communications, and provide inspiration and directions for the brand identity.

The components of the brand platform are:

### *Brand Values*

These are the principles that the city and its constituents believe in and live by. They are the values by which residents want their community to grow and be shared with others. It is possible that the community has never verbalized these thoughts until this process, even though they have probably been in play for a long time. They are frequently the reasons that a community is the way that it is. These may be the values that you hear repeated during local interviews and workshops because they reflect what the city does and does not want to become.

Community values may include the following:

- Affordability
- Authenticity
- Civic pride
- Community spirit
- Customer focus
- Environmental care
- Forward thinking
- Innovation
- Knowledge
- Patriotism
- Quality
- Reliability
- Safety
- Trust
- Volunteerism
- Welcoming

## Brand Vision

What is the vision held by city leaders for the future of the place in 5 or 20 years? What is the vision for the brand that is held by stakeholders? Is there a gap? Does it aspire to create a distinct competitive advantage or is it safe and bland?

The brand vision clarifies the high-level role that the brand will play in assisting the city achieve its long-term vision and goals. The brand vision should be connected to the city government's long-term vision, and also that of other major partners, otherwise there may be a serious disconnect. This vision provides partners with the directions on which to base future investment, growth and planning.

How will your vision for the brand fit with the community's values and vision? The brand vision should not be the sole province of the mayor or CEO, although they may be among the first to have strong ideas and perspectives as to what it should be. While considering this aspect, try to identify where the brand's energy and passion is likely to come from to attain the vision. Are there individuals, experiences and assets that are more ready to participate than others?

## Tangible Benefits

A brand cannot be created for a city that is devoid of attractions and assets – it must have credible physical assets and features that are valued by customers. These are the benefits that describe what the city has or does best. These may include interesting exhibits at museums, historical sites, easy access, sandy beaches, or wine tasting. Benefits such as these are often the easiest for competitors to claim or copy.

## Core Experiences

These are the broad categories representing key experiences in which the destination excels. These themes reflect its value proposition and competitive advantage in delivering outstanding customer moments. Examples of core experiences for tourism may include adventure, gardens, natural wonders, maritime heritage, cultural traditions or wellness.

### Emotional Benefits

Emotional benefits are the positive feelings that people receive from a place. While the tangible attributes may be enticing and important, they alone cannot create a deep relationship. Emotional benefits have the ability to change the way that people feel and connect with their deepest needs and desires. They should provide the state of mind that visitors are seeking, such as enrichment, romance, escape or adventure.

### Social Benefits

These are the benefits that reflect how people would like others to see them. At times they are called "bragging rights" and may relate to the celebrity, cache, and prestige of the place. They connect to one's self esteem and the positive recognition for being associated with this particular place.

### Personality

The role of personality is highly strategic, powerful and influential. It describes the brand in human terms. Places such as Nashville TN, Tucson AZ, or Silicon Valley CA each have their own individual character and personality. No matter which city you consider, it won't take long before you are describing it in the same terms that you would use to describe a person. Personality is extremely important in branding because it influences the words, colors, style and tone of voice we use in expressing it in marketing applications. Some of these personality traits may include:

- Adventurous
- Athletic
- Conservative
- Creative
- Cultured
- Down-to-earth

- Dynamic
- Energetic
- Exiting
- Free-spirited
- Fun
- Glamorous
- Industrious
- Innovative

- Intelligent
- Laid back
- Natural
- Optimistic
- Patriotic
- Sexy
- Sophisticated
- Warm

## Brand Credentials

Have you noticed how people like to patronize restaurants that have been favorably reviewed by a critic or order a wine that has won many awards? And have you seen the boost that an Oscar can give to a movie? Well, the same principle applies to cities.

Credentials, whether they evolve from association with an event, famous person, or favorable review, can give customers a satisfying peace of mind and level of trust that make it easier to choose them over alternatives. Providing credentials that give customers and prospects reasons to believe a city's positioning serves to strengthen the Destination Promise™. Brand credentials are particularly useful in destination marketing where the prospective visitor is purchasing an intangible that cannot be tested or examined before their arrival.

Andy Levine, President of Development Counsellors International, is a firm believer in the value of the credible, third-party endorsement. "If *Money* magazine says you're a great place to live, that means more than if you say it. If a corporation says you're a great place to do business, that's more credible than your ad. If you look at the two greatest brands in economic development, it's Silicon Valley and the Research Triangle. Neither was created through fancy logos; it was what the media and corporate executives said about them."

Brand credentials or "reasons to believe" help test and bullet-proof the Destination Promise™. Be sure to consider them during the planning phase to ensure that your brand proposition is realistic and can offer a defendable point of difference. Brand credentials may include:

- Achievements
- Awards
- Historical facts
- Intellectual property
- Movie location
- Site of a major event e.g. the Olympics, Little League World Series, etc.

- Media acknowledgements
- Prestige of other customers
- Quotes from famous people or experts
- Significant sites e.g. the Baseball Hall of Fame, birthplace of a President
- Subject of a book

### Brand Essence

The brand essence of a community is the DNA code from which the brand's narrative can evolve. This is the basic building block or glue that informs and holds together all brand experiences and messages. In the case of Astoria OR its rich maritime heritage inspires its brand essence: great maritime stories. This in turn is woven through its architecture, streetscapes, visitor experiences and economic development programs.

## Brand Associations

Brand associations are the attributes (positive, negative, and neutral) that come to mind when people are exposed to the brand name, tagline, symbols, or elements of a place. They amount to what your audiences know about the community and how they feel about investing time and money in it. Associations influence how we "file" and recall what we know about it. A city should aspire to have its positive attributes come to mind and be translated into highly valued benefits by its customers. For instance, the mention of New York City may instantly bring to mind dozens of the city's places, events, people, and activities, as well as being crowded, noisy, exciting, and a host of other descriptions. For most people, New York City has a richly painted canvas in their minds, even if they have never visited there.

On the other hand, associations can work in reverse. Consumers may think of a word, need, product, benefit or feeling, which immediately triggers them to think of a city name. Achieving this level of positive name associations is the ultimate goal. To use the New York City example again, the thought of "outstanding theater" or "big city excitement" may bring New York City immediately to mind. The trick, of course, is to ensure that the destination is associated with positive benefits and preferably those that are integral to your brand identity. You don't want to be the place that comes to mind when pollution, crime, litter, rip-offs, bad traffic, or the phrase "tourist trap" are mentioned.

## It Takes an Emotional Edge

Consider some of the world's most powerful consumer brands like Nike, Victoria's Secret, and Disney. If these brands were based only on their physical elements, they would be much the same as their competitors. Instead, they have differentiated themselves by connecting with the emotional needs of customers, creating strong bonds, expectations, trust and intangible rewards. The reward for Nike's customers may be a sense of achievement, and Victoria's Secret promises self-expression and confidence.

I really like what fellow Australian, Geoff Ayling said in *Rapid Response Advertising,* "There is only one reason why people have ever bought from you in the past, and why they will ever buy from you in the future, and that is because they want to change the way they feel. It's that simple."[20]

While Disney theme park guests connect through family freedom, Las Vegas is about adult freedom, and Reno NV is similar but with a sense of adventure of the outdoors surrounding the city. Unlike many consumer products,

cities have the opportunity to form rich and meaningful connections with their visitors. We become totally immersed and surrounded by them, sometimes for several days, and this can profoundly influence and stimulate our senses.

When choosing a city to visit, people are often seeking a particular emotional state of mind. Some places make the mistake of simply offering them lists of local Chamber of Commerce and CVB members and images of their generic physical attributes. The feelings that prospective visitors desire are not captured in a list of places, attractions or facilities. These are simply the *features* of the place and rarely connect on an emotional level. The next time you happen to be walking around a resort, historic town, winery, or along a forest trail, look at people around you. You will recognize that everyone you see is there to create or maintain a positive emotional state by feeling better in some way.

The number one challenge for city marketers is to understand and connect with this desire to feel good (or better) because that's the overwhelming hot button or trigger for all destination-related decisions.

Nigel Morgan and Annette Pritchard in their book *Destination Branding* also make the point that, "The choice of vacation (or getaway) destination is a significant lifestyle indicator for today's aspirational consumers. The places where they choose to spend their increasingly squeezed vacation time and hard earned income have to be emotionally appealing with high conversational and celebrity value."[21]

We only have to look at the growing popularity of spas, luxury resorts and places associated with celebrities to confirm this trend. Also note the influence of television programs and films in the increased awareness and esteem for some places. Recent television and films have placed the spotlight on Providence RI, Boston MA, Honolulu HI, and Orange County CA. These have always been popular destinations, but the added media attention gives them added cache and marks them as even more desirable places to be associated with.

Miami has benefited greatly from television productions shot on location in the city. "*All Miami, all the time* is my mantra," commented William D. Talbert III, CDME, President and CEO of the Greater Miami Convention & Visitors Bureau. "No CVB's budget can accomplish that goal by itself: and for Miami, movies like *Miami Vice* and a top-rated weekly TV program such as *CSI: Miami* help keep Miami's name top of mind. Both showcase the excitement, glamour and beauty – both natural and man-made – of our area, precisely our goal in reinforcing Miami's brand identity in worldwide markets," Talbert concluded.

**Climb the Brand Value Pyramid**

The brand benefits pyramid (Figure 3) demonstrates the importance of the brand to customers and the effect that emotional and social benefits have upon them. All brand marketers should aim to be associated with the qualities at the peak of the pyramid. Occupying this position makes it difficult for other communities to occupy this same space and offer exactly the same value. This could be called the 'Holy Grail' for destination marketers because it is the ultimate positioning for those who want to rise above the many other places that are only relying on their physical attributes and features. The closer to the peak of the triangle that the city goes in delivering value through emotional benefits the more it will be differentiated and the more firmly it will bond with visitors in a way that will be extremely hard for others to match.

A destination engaged in a competitive tussle with another location should try to move up the pyramid in order to establish an emotional benefit that the other place cannot easily claim.

While emotional benefits start to appear on the third step of the pyramid, it is when they bond with the customer's personal values and beliefs at the pinnacle that they are their most potent. A person's motivation for visiting the city is closely aligned with their personal values and beliefs or because it makes an important social statement about them. It may offer heightened esteem with friends, family and colleagues. For instance, some places afford strong bragging rights and a high level of celebrity, such as visiting The Hamptons NY, Newport RI, Beverly Hills CA, or South Beach FL. Similarly, Colorado ski resorts such as Aspen,

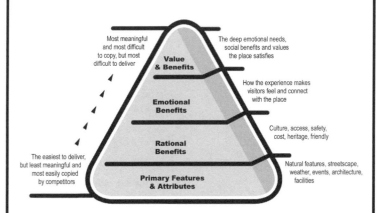

**Figure 3: Brand Benefits Pyramid**

Telluride and Vail have strong celebrity status. These places may reflect very well on those who visit them, can be a source of admiration among peers, conferring "social benefits" through the level of esteem that they afford those who visit them.

When cities occupy a position at the peak, they are able to enjoy greater loyalty and positive word of mouth than places on the lower levels of the pyramid. They are also more likely to command premium prices and can usually generate more media coverage, investment, and goodwill than most of their competitors.

## Seeing Things from Your Customer's Perspective

The more that a city learns about its target customers and their needs and desires, the better it can connect with them. The following are some of the deep-felt needs that represent the emotional connections on which to base the city's positioning, communications and experiences.

- To attract the opposite (or same) sex
- To be entertained
- To be indulgent
- To be informed
- To be in style or fashionable
- To be successful
- To become more fit and healthy
- To challenge oneself
- To connect with people
- To escape (many things)
- To express love and romance
- To feel like a good parent
- To feel opulent or sophisticated
- To feel pampered
- To feel superior or first
- To gain confidence
- To increase enjoyment
- To 'keep up with the Joneses'
- To make a better world (volunteering)
- To pursue a passion
- To reward oneself
- To understand others

Whatever benefits are selected, they must provide a competitive edge and offer a compelling reason for selecting your city over another. When two places share the same attributes, it is the emotional and social benefits that will be the "tie breaker" and provide the distinctive point of difference.

More and more destinations are responding to the trend for short breaks and the emotional reward of escaping everyday stress. Central to the brand identity of Palm Springs and Desert Resorts CA is escaping the worries and pace of everyday life, while Toledo OH invites people in other nearby metropolitan areas to *Do what refreshes you*, and Bellingham WA offers Seattle's residents the opportunity to escape the stresses of big city living for *A Refreshing Change*.

Many coastal communities use their beaches as the mainstay of their marketing to differentiate themselves. But all beaches are not the same. What does it feel like to escape a crowded city and sit under a palm tree on a broad, white sand, deserted beach with just the sound of the gulls and the pounding surf? What emotions and sensations does it stimulate? Is this different to the experience and sensations on a beach lined with high-rise apartments, restaurants and night clubs, music, and boutique shops? Should they all be communicating the same benefits, images and words?

So often we see the same imagery for all types of beach experience, missing the distinctive promise of how each place can make you feel and how it's different. The benefits from all coastal communities and beaches are not the same, as you can discover on a short drive along the California coast from the casual upscale escapes and "active relaxation" of San Diego North, to the inspiration of the artistic talent in Laguna Beach, to the beach-plus experience of Costa Mesa, and Santa Monica presenting "the essence of California lifestyle." Each is clearly differentiating itself, including offshore Catalina Island which invites us to escape to "the island of romance."

## Creating the Destination Promise™

The Destination Promise™ is a series of carefully formulated statements that guide everything the DMO and destination do in building the brand (Figure 4). When completed it is the Destination Promise™ and not the tagline that you follow. This is the foundation for all future marketing programs and should have an influence on every marketing, organizational, and development decision. Its creation should not be rushed and must be very carefully crafted. Every word has to earn its place. Critical words should explode with meaning. The Destination Promise™ needs to be considered from both the customer's point of view, as well as from the perspective of residents, partners, and stakeholders. It outlines the key audience, tangible and emotional benefits, and states what sets it apart and why only this location is capable of satisfying the audience in this way. The Destination Promise™ is formulated after thorough analysis of the destination's strengths from the demand perspective i.e. considering the needs and wants of prospective customers and the supply perspective i.e. the ability of the place to sustain their delivery.

> **The Destination Promise™ is the foundation for all future marketing programs and should have an influence on every marketing, organizational, and development decision.**

## The Importance of the Destination Promise™

The basic tenet of a brand is that it is a promise that will be fulfilled. Our experience in building destination brands has shown us the need to move beyond the traditional positioning statement and create a precise community promise that will lead its brand behavior. This has evolved to what we call the Destination Promise™, clarifying what the city wants to be known for, and detailing what is required to make it happen. Importantly, it compels the DMO and its partners to consider why only their community among its competitors can satisfy customers in this way.

**Figure 4: The Destination Promise is the
Beacon for all DMO Programs**

Time and again, designing the Destination Promise™ in a collaborative and research-based manner has proven successful in helping stakeholders abandon their self-interest and parochialism for more customer-centric thinking. Importantly, the Destination Promise™ acts as a reality check to ensure the place is capable of fulfilling its commitment. It also considers whether there are brand credentials or "reasons to believe" that provide evidence to support the claim.

## What Does a Destination Promise™ Look Like?

Step Two of the *7A Process* culminates in formulating the Destination Promise™. The first component to be created is the positioning statement. This statement is comprised of several short sentences that concisely summarize what distinguishes the place and spells out why the city is the best available option for target customers. This concise statement sets the strategic language and roots for the future management of the brand. The following is an example of a Destination Promise™ for a fictitious place called Smithville, Colorado.

*Smithville represents Colorado's foremost combination of mountain and cultural experiences. It has dramatic scenery, small town charm, spas, outstanding restaurants and a year-round cultural calendar. Only Smithville uniquely combines mountain tranquility, a thriving colony of renowned artists, and a national historic district with experiences that enrich, rejuvenate and provide spiritual satisfaction for visitors.*

*Our community is dedicated to preserving and enhancing our natural and cultural environment, and providing our visitors with outstanding and satisfying experiences that are enriching and rejuvenating.*

*In Colorado, only Smithville has such an outstanding combination of mountain, historical, cultural experiences as the following accolades and achievements illustrate.*

- *Smithville is designated as a "Trail Town USA" by the American Hiking Society because of its 20 miles of pedestrian, bicycle and equestrian trails.*

- *Smithville has been consistently praised by America's leading active lifestyle, culture, and adventure magazines as one of the nations premier mountain biking, snowboarding, running, and artistic retreats.*

- *The Peak Art Festival each year attracts over 8,000 artists and enthusiasts from around the world.*

- *The historic buildings along Silver Street are identified as being among the finest examples of 1880's architecture in the state by the Colorado Centenary Association.*

## Testing the Promise

Once you have a draft of the Destination Promise™, it should be tested with stakeholders, and ideally with customers as well. You are not looking for them to rewrite it, but to assess it for clarity and believability. If necessary, it can then be fine-tuned to enhance its relevance, appeal, and content.

The Destination Promise™ should be considered in terms of six factors:

- *Believable* – Will prospects believe the underlying proposition?

- *Differentiating* – Will it really make the city stand apart in a way that is meaningful?

- *Enduring* – Is it deliverable and will it be sustainable for years to come?

- *Motivating* – Will it be an inspiring and enticing proposition?

- *Relevant* – Will it matter to a sufficient number of customers?

- *Strategic* – Does it fit with the vision, strategic objectives, and community values?

## What Happens if You Break the Promise?

If the Destination Promise™, is not fulfilled it is highly unlikely that the brand will attain the desired outcomes expected of it. Some of the negative impacts may include:

- Visitors reducing their length of stay, minimizing their spending, deciding not to return, or spreading negative word of mouth.

- Staff and partners considering it unimportant or ineffective, and a downward spiral sets in that undermines the Promise and the brand.

- Residents and local leaders reducing their support for the brand and the DMO to the extent that it may be years before enthusiasm for another similar effort can be considered.

## Questions

Important questions to be answered during Step Two are:

- What are the city's areas of competitive advantage?

- What are the strengths, key benefits and experiences that should be most associated with the city?

- What are the components of the brand platform?

- What positioning should be claimed?

- What are the core experiences that underpin the Destination Promise™?

- Have you tested the Destination Promise™?

## CHAPTER EIGHT

# Step Three: Architecture and Alignment – What Are the Brand's Relationships?

While Step Three concentrates on the brand architecture and alignment, they are issues that should be considered during every stage of the planning process.

The brand architecture defines the relationships between the city's various internal locations, entities, and experiences within its boundaries. These may also be referred to as sub-brands. The overall brand architecture can be compared to a family tree, because it illustrates the relationships between elements as if they were the individuals and generations of a family.

Now that you have completed your analysis and are finalizing your Destination Promise™ you can decide whether the architecture should be based on an overarching brand. An overarching brand is the overall, high-level brand that embraces all elements of the community and forms a unifying umbrella for the city's marketing entities. It may also be referred to as a place brand or location brand because it is intended to embrace all marketing aspects of the place. If you opt for an overarching brand, you must seriously consider whether it will have sufficient potency to be relevant and meaningful to all audiences.

Among the benefits of an overarching brand are that it:

- Provides a unifying framework through which all entities responsible for marketing any aspect of the city (tourism, relocation, students, economic development, etc.) can present it in a consistent and compelling manner.

- Captures the agreed superior benefits and personality in a way that is integrated and consistent across all communications.

- Engages partners in reinforcing what is distinctive about the place.

- Generates synergy and stretches marketing dollars thanks to the focused messages of all stakeholders – many voices, one message.

- Eliminates the dissonance that may occur when partners and other entities are conveying different or contradictory messages about the city.

A challenge for destination marketers is that "the same physical area has to be sold for different reasons to diverse groups with different needs, and at the same time. For example, within the leisure tourism market, audiences exist at local, regional, national and international levels and the brand must appeal to all of these groups."[22] A city may also be projecting itself on the basis of its beaches to tourism markets, and at the same time to other audiences on the basis of its emerging high tech industries, educated workforce, and available industrial sites.

When it comes to understanding how individual geographic locations within the area can relate to the overall city or regional brand, the family metaphor is most appropriate. When we observe members of the family together we see that they are different and independent individuals. However, we can see a family resemblance in each of them because they share the family DNA. It is this commonality that creates the opportunity for individual locations to benefit from the city or regional brand if this shared DNA or brand essence can be adopted and communicated in a way that is relevant and meaningful for their individual audiences.

When defining the brand you must always be conscious of the relationships and alignment with other entities and places within its boundaries, including:

1. Tourism-related entities and marketing partners within the destination such as hotels, transportation, and attractions.
2. Locations such as other cities, neighborhoods and geographical features within the destination.
3. The relationships with the entities responsible for the city's marketing portfolio, including tourism, economic development, relocation, inward investment, student recruitment, and even the identity of the area's products.
4. County, state, and provincial brands, if appropriate.

The first two are almost always present and can be accommodated relatively easily, but it is the third that is more complex and usually presents the greatest difficulties. While in many cases, it is preferable for the tourism and economic development brands to share the same brand essence or DNA, it is not always possible or advisable.

> **While in many cases, it is preferable for the tourism and economic development brands to share the same brand essence or DNA, it is not always possible or advisable.**

Sometimes, the marketing materials of cities (particularly government agencies), often coming from within the same building, can look as if they were produced by different cities. While the messages from these various agencies don't have to be identical because of their different audiences and their needs, it should be apparent that they are referring to the same place. When promoting the lifestyle and visitor strengths of the city, economic development marketers should project the city as prescribed in the brand strategy for tourism, and not makeup their own descriptions.

Each of the city's marketing entities must employ messages that are fine-tuned to their particular audiences and, when appropriate, use common words, phrases, descriptions, images, colors and designs. Adopting these brand elements can prove far more effective than simply striving to create the same positioning, logo and tagline for all entities. This does not mean that one brand positioning can be expected to fit all messages and applications. Each entity must eventually focus on its own target audiences for tourism, student recruitment, economic development and the particular needs and benefits that each seeks.

The needs and desires of customer groups vary within tourism and economic development marketing. Consequently, the positioning may also need to be adapted to convey the strongest proposition for such diverse needs as those of domestic and international visitors, corporations searching for new head office locations, or group travel planners.

There may be the need for some fine-tuning even within the tourism brand itself. The Orlando/Orange County Convention & Visitors Bureau found this when their research indicated the need to position the city differently for the meetings market than for the leisure market. Orlando's strong image had been shaped by its outstanding theme parks, that include Disney World, Universal Studios, Wet 'n Wild, and SeaWorld. However, research indicated that their positioning for the meetings market needed a more sophisticated look portraying Orlando as a more "grown up" city. The CVB found the need to present high-end adult and business-oriented amenities.[23]

## The Search for an Overarching Brand

While there may be strong reasons for creating one overarching brand, it is not always possible to define a brand platform that will be strong and relevant to the diverse marketing needs of all local entities. It can be done, but too often the result is based on a series of compromises that moves the focus off customer hot buttons and onto points of commonality that are not distinctive, meaningful or compelling to any customers. In other cases it may be politics and turf protection that work against the effort.

Andy Levine, president of Development Counsellors International, supports this view, "I've noticed a major movement to try to come up with a common brand for multiple entities within a region or city. But the needs of a corporate executive who is trying to set up a regional office are completely different than a leisure traveler or meeting planner. Every time I've seen it done, you end up with a very bland logo or themeline; it's very hard to find something that does double duty."

A successful overarching brand requires a brand essence (remember the DNA analogy) on which the positioning and brand platform can be based so that it will be highly valued by the key target audiences of the entities marketing the city. When places start reaching for less potent propositions on which to base the brand, simply to create "something we can all use" they are on their way to creating an anemic brand. This leads toward diluted positioning based on a very weak and at times irrelevant point of difference such as friendliness, service, lifestyle or community pride. All of which are usually entry-level requirements, not points of differentiation that are enticing to outside customers.

Durham NC and Astoria-Warrenton OR are two cities who are successfully developing overarching brands because their brand DNA resonates with their key audiences and throughout their communities.

Reyn Bowman, president of Durham Convention and Visitors Bureau, highlights the need for special care when focusing on the city's many customer groups. He says, "The overarching Durham brand has been embraced and activated by groups across the community as diverse as our tourism partners, universities, neighborhoods and dance companies because in the process of distilling it accurately, we identified elements which both external and internal stakeholders valued highly. We struck the right balance because it is now coming to life across the community and resonating positively with our key external audiences."

Through extra research, consultation and creativity Reyn was able to encourage community support and enthusiasm for the brand. The primary tagline for Durham, *Where great things happen*™ was designed to encourage the whole community to adapt it to better connect with their particular audiences. For example, with prior approval partners can substitute other words for the word "*things*" in the tagline to reflect specific Durham strengths. Variations might include *Where great dance happens* or *Where great education happens* or *Where great discoveries happen*. Durham-based Research Triangle Park dovetailed its new brand and tagline perfectly by adopting the line *The future of great ideas*.

Canada's Banff – Lake Louise also encourages partners to create variations on the main tagline, *Celebrate life*. Partners can choose from fourteen extensions that include, "Skiing," "Dining," "Exploring" and "Genuinely" to clarify and reinforce the promise and experiences.

Todd Scott, Astoria's Community Development Director, explains his city's overarching brand, "We're known for our rich maritime heritage, part of this is our reputation as a center for commercial fishing and shipping services. We're also known for our port atmosphere and historic riverfront, so we also present those images to visitors. And people come to Astoria and Warrenton to go to the beach and watch storms," Scott said. "Everything we do now, whether its tourism, whether it's economic development, whatever it is, can fall under the umbrella of this brand with the tagline, *The Spirit of the Columbia*. This is who we are as a community."

There is no hard and fast rule regarding an overarching brand. Some places choose to adopt the tourism brand identity because it suits their strategy of projecting the lifestyle of the place and this may also be central to their economic development strategy. It depends upon the objectives, local politics and scale of the city's non-tourism marketing efforts. We have found that the larger the community or destination, the more difficult the task of defining and gaining consensus for a sustainable overarching brand.

## Overarching Brands Demand Customer Focus and Collaboration

Destination brands are strengthened when there is clarity and agreement regarding what the place represents, irrespective of who is saying it. Ideally, the brand will capture the character and personality in a way that can be integrated and consistent across the city's marketing portfolio.

To be most effective, an overarching brand should be adaptable by city marketers to suit their particular target audiences. Where commonality exists between the various messages, the individual efforts can gain wider coverage and be more impactful. Achieving success takes a very concerted effort, and may require an extended period simply to get the right participants around the table and to agree on collaborating.

Over recent years, a number of cities, such as Hartford CT and Richmond VA have been addressing the challenges of creating overarching brands.

Hartford recognized the need to build their overarching brand through broad regional engagement. They formed a 12-organization consortium to develop a brand identity that would communicate the economic renaissance underway. The group represented economic development, tourism, the convention center, the arts, Office of the Mayor and other organizations. It led the branding initiative that embraced the 36-town Hartford region using the tagline *New England's Rising Star* to unify the messages of all organizations.[24]

Similarly, the *Historic Richmond Region — Easy to Love* brand strategy was developed through a partnership of nine local organizations including the Greater Richmond Chamber of Commerce, Retail Merchants Association, Richmond International Airport, and the Virginia Biotechnology Research Park. Many of these organizations, including Richmond International Airport, have incorporated the ...*Easy to Love* tagline into their marketing and adopted messages appropriate to their customer communications.[25]

Representing eight cities and the county, Palm Springs Desert Resorts Convention Visitors Association (PSDRCVA) had the challenge of ensuring that local cities within its boundaries embraced the brand and were able to play a meaningful role in its delivery. "The Palm Springs Desert Resorts brand promises the visitor the opportunity to enjoy the fun, glamour, and beauty of an authentic, relaxing California resort while escaping from the worries and pace of everyday life," said a CVA spokesperson. PSDRCVA asked each city to endorse the brand promise and to then concentrate on what they were famous for, whether Hollywood history, mountains, or big-horn sheep. "Some of them have their own marketing message, but it is compatible and consistent with the brand promise. They are all selling from the same script," explained the spokesperson.[26] This is similar to our analogy of all partners being part of the same family and sharing a common DNA. Here it is *the fun, glamour, and beauty of an authentic California resort.*

In many cases, tourism is the most visible marketing effort on behalf of a city or region. The quality and visibility of this effort usually has a strong influence in shaping perceptions of a city's overarching brand image. When they were each developing their brand strategies, the cities of Grants Pass on the Rogue River OR and Santa Rosa County FL agreed that among their best small business relocation candidates were people who had previously visited as a tourist. They reasoned that once someone has a positive experience of the community with the state of mind of a visitor, they are much more open to the thought of relocating their business or family to the area.

## Questions

Important questions to be answered during Step Three are:

- Is an overarching brand appropriate?

- Will the proposed brand be in harmony with the brands of the community's other marketing entities, e.g. economic development, tourism, recruitment? Does it need to be?

- Is it clear how geographic locations and tourism partners within the area relate to the city brand and will be able to use it in a meaningful way?

- Are there partner-related issues and opportunities to keep in mind?

## CHAPTER NINE

# Step Four: Articulate – How Will the Brand Be Expressed?

Now that you are armed with the brand platform and Destination Promise™, the focus moves to the design of the visual and verbal identity systems that will touch the senses. Here the emphasis shifts from the left-brain logic that has driven the brand planning, to right-brain innovation and creativity which inspires the brand's designs and communications.

## Designing the Verbal Identity

The verbal identity includes the brand name, tagline, copy style, brand stories, and key elements that make the brand's language distinctive, enticing, and informative. It is not uncommon for the power of words to be initially overlooked in favor of the color and visual enticement of the logo, yet words are among the most potent and affordable branding tools at your disposal. By consistently using carefully chosen words, phrases and stories that best support the Destination Promise™, you can cost-effectively build the brand.

## The Brand Name

The face of a brand is its name. It has often been said that being introduced to a brand is like meeting a person. Their name is extremely important: because it's how we remember them, store information, and refer to them. It is as if there is a little filing cabinet in our brains where we keep everything relevant to that name. When we hear of San Antonio TX, we can readily recall the many pieces of information, thoughts and feelings that we have assembled about it over the years, even if we have never been there.

On the other hand, if we hear about Springfield TX, we have to be careful that we don't confuse it with the information that we have stored about Springfield IL, Springfield OR, or Springfield MA. Hence, it is important – though not always possible – to have a name that is distinctive and will not be confused with others. At last count there are 33 Washington counties in the USA, and there are more cities named Springfield than just about any other in the USA. Sometimes the city's name may not be ideal for marketing purposes, but may be impossible to change because of local attachment to it. Unlike the producers of consumer brands that usually engage a naming specialist and research the most appropriate names for their products, cities already have names that may have been used for centuries. While residents may be emotionally tied to the city name, it may not present the city in the best light to external audiences. Additionally, some cities have names that are difficult to pronounce or remember. Skaneateles NY and Skamokawa WA can be difficult for non-locals to pronounce at first, let alone try to remember or spell.

The citizens of White Settlement TX recently voted 2,388 to 219 in a ballot initiative to hold onto their heritage and not change the city name to West Settlement. The city received its name in the 1840s when it was the lone village of white pioneers amid several American Indian encampments in the Fort Worth area, of the Texas Republic Territory. This ballot initiative failed despite city leaders informing residents that the name was confusing, misleading and had deterred companies from moving into this area of Fort Worth.[27] City leaders of Galveston TX were also confronted with the prospect of a name change for the city and rejected the idea of changing the city name to Galveston Island.[28]

Some cities have changed their destination name for marketing purposes, as well as the name of the organization leading their marketing efforts. Once known only as a military town, Norfolk VA coined the name New Norfolk for its marketing campaign to draw attention to the extensive revitalization that has occurred, although the official name of the city will remain Norfolk. Lebanon OR refers to itself as LebanonCity in economic development marketing so that it can be distinguished from the other 24 cities in the USA named Lebanon. Colorado Springs is now marketed as "Experience Colorado Springs at Pike's Peak." Terry Sullivan, the bureau's president and CEO said, "We have built our image around experiencing Colorado Springs in everything that we do, and this now includes our organization's name, Experience Colorado Springs at Pike's Peak CVB."[29]

Some of the names and terms associated with a place can be among its most valuable assets, and need to be strongly protected. This is exemplified by the Huntington Beach CVB, which trademarked *"Surf City* USA™" to capitalize on the city's 50-year-old California surfing heritage and its place in American popular culture. Claiming the name might not seem like such a big deal, since people have been calling it "Surf City" for decades. But the move touched a nerve in the San Francisco Bay area, where Santa Cruz claims that it is the real Surf City. The decades-old rivalry made good fodder for radio and television shows. Today, the name *"Surf City* USA™" resides securely in Huntington Beach.[30]

## Tagline

A tagline is a word or short phrase that captures the spirit of the Destination Promise™. The tagline can be a tease, a short descriptor, a call to action, or an explanation and succinctly stated usually in no more than five words. You may choose to create one to support the city name, although this is not essential.

Sometimes a tagline is referred to as a slogan. However a slogan, typically developed specifically for an advertising campaign has a limited use. A tagline is created for indefinite use in a variety of applications.

Whenever I see a tagline, I find myself asking "Where did it come from? Was this simply a bright idea that somebody had, or is it an expression of something deeper where the city has a strategic intent and is trying to address a specific objective?" Too often, I fear that the former is the case. The tagline should promise or infer something that can be valued by customers and which can actually be delivered to them. It should be more than simply a clever line that carries no clear meaning or value.

Marcia McMillen, president of McMillen Creative says, "A brand platform based on differentiation helps communities avoid the trap of common taglines such as *Gateway to ...*, *Best Kept Secret ..* or *Small Town Charm with Big City Amenities*. They sound the same and they look the same, because the communities are only looking at themselves instead of at competitors and customer needs."

Too many destination taglines like these are a meaningless assembly of words that have emerged from a brainstorming session without considering their relationship to a promise, positioning, competitors, customer benefits, or whether it is a credible and deliverable experience. Because a tagline or slogan sounds appealing to a group of locals doesn't mean it will stand up well to the scrutiny of the marketplace.

To assess the appropriateness of a tagline, the following checklist of eight factors may be useful:

- It must be short, usually less than five words

- It must not be the same as or similar to that used by other places

- It should not have negative connotations

- It must capture and dramatize the spirit of the Destination Promise™

- It hints at a reward, benefit or experience that customers value and can expect

- It is credible, sustainable and appropriate

- It is easy to remember and repeat
- It works with and enhances the logo

It's a good idea to check with the United States Trademark and Patents Office Website (www.uspto.gov/main/trademarks.htm) to assess the availability of specific terms. This site enables you to conduct a preliminary search for similar phrases and words that may already be trademarked and in use. We also recommend extensive online searches to assess whether the tagline is already in use or registered. As soon as your Brand Advisory Group officially endorses the tagline, steps should commence immediately to formally register it as a trademark. There are always entities and individuals out there who may knowingly or unknowingly decide to use your tagline. A case in point is Las Vegas' tagline, *What happens here, stays here.* Over the past few years Las Vegas has spent more than US $730,000 on legal fees defending its ownership of the line against entrepreneurs wanting to sell everything from underwear to video games.[31]

There are many words and terms that have been so over-used or misused in taglines and advertising that they have lost much of their potency. They are like wallpaper – people have seen them so often that they take very little notice of them and place them into the realm of "advertising-speak." Others are devalued because they lack credibility and because the reader suspects that the proposition is an exaggeration or simply cannot be true.

On two adjoining pages in a popular travel magazine, I recently saw seven small advertisements for destinations containing eight of the following words and phrases. Three of the seven places were using several of the same words in their tagline and headline. These overused words include:

- Discover
- Discover yourself
- Enjoy

- Explore
- Friendly
- Gateway to

- Historical
- Natural
- Relaxing

- The best
- The center of
- Welcoming

I'm not saying that you should never use these words, after all *Super, Natural British Columbia* is one of the most enduring taglines of the past twenty years. Seattle's recently announced tagline *metronatural* is another very creative and probably appropriate expression. But you must be innovative and make a strong statement when using these words by applying them in unexpected and clever ways.

## Key Words and Phrases

Just as the term "talking points" has found its way into our vocabulary to describe the words, phrases, and sentences that politicians consistently use to get their messages across, each city also needs its own talking points or key messages. This helps keep all staff, partners, and stakeholders "on message" when speaking or writing about the city. These words and phrases should consistently appear in all appropriate brochures, Websites, speeches, and presentations.

## Brand Stories

Since people first sat around a fire and recounted their hunting expeditions, stories have been used as a means of entertainment, engagement, instruction, and communication. Today, by tapping into the power of storytelling, brand marketers can inject greater meaning and emotion into their brands. The power of storytelling has often been undervalued in tourism and destination marketing. As marketers we can learn a lot from the words of famed defense attorney Gerry Spence from Wyoming who maintains "winning is just a matter of finding the right story." He frequently starts his courtroom summation by saying, "Now, let me tell you a story."

The stories, anecdotes, legends, and myths that are associated with a community make it all the more meaningful and attractive to us. Stories can be the catalyst and the entry point for deeper emotional connections. The best brand stories recall and reinforce the essence or spirit of the place. They can be informative, inspirational or motivational and can be varied according to the audience you are trying to influence.

Of course, some places have better and more engaging stories than other places. Some are larger than fiction. Imagine the tales that the streets of Tombstone AZ can tell about Wyatt Earp, or the yarns of miners in Leadville CO, or the ghost stories of Frederick MD.

Robert Uguccioni, Executive Director of Pennsylvania's Pocono Mountain Visitors Bureau believes that delivering a brand promise through its 'core story' is a strategic priority for destinations. Uguccioni said, "Look at any powerful brand, you will find a "core story" at the heart of it. Stories are a fundamental way that human beings communicate with each other. Our members devoted two days engaged in creative exercises that lead to the crafting of a core story for the Pocono Mountains brand that would bring our promise to life. The sessions also made our organization very aware that without taking the brand promise and translating that into everyday acts of brand ambassadorship, the entire branding initiative would remain surface level."

Wherever possible, brand stories should be woven into the brand messages and experiences. They should relate closely to your brand credentials, which you identified as the "reasons to believe" in the Destination Promise™. A city's most engaging stories might be based on:

- Achievements
- Architecture and buildings
- Events and incidents

- Famous visitors
- Founders and ancestors
- History

- Local products and indus-
  tries
- Natural environment
- Residents and leaders

- Sporting events
- Unusual or unique charac-
  teristics
- Values and philosophies

They should be the kind of anecdotes that fit easily into the con-
versations that visitors and residents would have with each other. All
cities have their own stories, for example the origins of the Ford Mo-
tor Company in Dearborn MI, the railroad heritage of Altoona PA
or the buildings designed by world-famous architects in Columbus
IN. Some are unique to them, while some, like the Underground
Railroad, The Oregon Trail, or the Pennsylvania Dutch Country are
shared with many other cities and regions.

Cities have the ability to bring their themes or stories to life
many times during the destination experience. Whether standing
in a place made famous by a city's favorite son, marveling at his
achievements in the local museum, walking a street named for him,
or listening to a guide who knew him, cities have near limitless
opportunities to connect with visitors and to reinforce their stories.
Simply walking around some places can make you feel as though
you are part of the story. For example, walking into an encampment
of Civil War re-enactors near Gettysburg PA can make you feel
as though you are "inside" some of the stories that have defined
the community (and the nation). When the stories truly engage
visitors, they are a powerful force for delivering outstanding brand
experiences.

Interesting narratives that engage and excite prospective customers can become the differentiating factors if that community is
similar to competitors on other dimensions. Selma AL has been able
to use the inspiring stories of its citizen's involvement in the Civil
Rights Movement to set it apart. For example, visitors to the city's
National Voting Rights Museum can hear the fascinating first-hand

accounts of guides who were veterans of the civil rights movement. How can you bring your stories to life?

## Design the Visual Identity

The visual identity system includes the logo, logotype, fonts, color palette, photo images, symbols, and the distinctive look or designs that express the brand. It may also extend to the designs for special applications such as buildings, office interiors, furnishings, vehicles, uniforms, merchandise, street banners, signage, trade show booths, and more.

## Logo

The term "logo" is derived from *logotype*, which originated from *Logos*, a Greek term for "word." The logo or mark is a core element of the brand identity and is inspired by the Destination Promise™. Logos are trademarks comprising custom-lettered words, symbols, illustrations, emblems, or a combination of these elements. The logo is created to trigger and aid recall of positive brand associations and to convey meaning about the place. However, it may only have real meaning for those who are already familiar with the place or product.

Along with taglines, logo development tends to absorb a disproportionate amount of attention and energy from branding committees and some local constituents. I am not saying that a logo (or tagline for that matter) is not important, but you must be careful not to end up with the proverbial "camel designed by a committee." Many city brands would be much stronger if more attention had been paid to other aspects of the strategy, particularly those associated with accurately communicating and delivering its experiences and promise.

Despite having worked on logo designs for many months, the recommended design may not always be greeted enthusiastically when people first see it. Don't be dispirited. Customers, and stakeholders for that matter, don't always immediately understand the meaning of a design. Even citizens of the USA didn't immediately grasp the meaning of the nation's flag, the Stars and Stripes, when it was first introduced. Betsy Ross simply created an interesting design featuring stars on a piece of fabric. It took many more years of tumult and triumphs to build its meaning and relevance in the hearts of Americans. Logos can face similar challenges. They sometimes need time to connect and resonate.

We have all seen those logos where a city has tried to cram everything into a design in an attempt to not offend anyone. The result is a confusing collage of city features that are rendered meaningless, particularly when they are reduced in size. Another mistake that some cities make is conducting a competition within the community or among students to design their new logo. It may be free or cheap, but believe me they usually get what they pay for.

Some of the criteria to use in deciding on a logo are:

- Does it capture and dramatize the spirit of the Destination Promise™?
- Can it be reduced for small-scale applications?
- Is it suitable for use on merchandise?
- Will it reproduce well in black and white?
- Can it be confused with other logos?

To aid in final refinement and selection, test your three or four leading designs on prospective customers outside of the city. This can be accomplished by using a number of cost effective research techniques, including online surveys, focus groups, or intercept interviews. After the logo is selected, register it with the United States Trademarks and Patents Office.

## Logotype

This is the typeface only component of the logo or mark. It may comprise only the name of the community rather than include a symbol. The logotype may use an existing, commonly available font which can be altered slightly for a more tailored look, or it may be a design featuring customized calligraphy. A custom illustrated mark will be more costly than the logotype developed from an existing font.

## Color Palette

How would you feel walking onto an aircraft with a black interior? How do you react when you see a billboard with a red background? Colors can have a profound effect on our emotions and preferences. The selection of a color palette is an integral, yet under-utilized source of differentiation and communication by destinations. Different colors carry different meanings. They may include:

- Black      Power, dignity, serious, tradition, funereal
- Blue       Tranquility, healing, knowledge, integrity, power
- Brown      History, earthy, traditional
- Green      Nature, health, freshness, calm
- Pink       Feminine, soft, youthful
- Red        Passion, aggressive, strength, vitality, stop
- Turquoise  Calm, relaxation, soothing
- White      Pure, clean, refined, truthful
- Yellow     Cowardly, warning, youth, sunshine

When deciding on your color palette, consider the colors that are used by competitors. Avoid the dominant color that may already be associated with your leading competitors. Are there colors that are indigenous to the area? Astoria-Warrenton OR is effectively using a color pallet inspired by the labels of the salmon cans that were used by the old seafood canneries which once populated its shores.

## Fonts and Typography

Your selection of fonts and typography may be subtle, but they make a strong statement. Just think for a moment of the hundreds of places where customers will see your written words. Beyond the obvious logo, brochures and advertising, written words have a powerful influence in everything from stationery and Web pages to posters, name badges, and street signs.

Regardless of your budget, this can be one of the most cost-effective elements of an identity program. Ensure that the final selections support your brand positioning and personality. Software programs such as Word and WordPerfect provide easy access to a wide selection of fonts from which you can project your identity in everyday applications.

## Photography

High quality photography has the capacity to be one of the most potent and versatile elements in the brand toolkit, yet most communities under-invest in it. What sense does it make to pay top dollar for printing and advertising only to project inferior and off-brand images? Instead, present the community's special sense of place, benefits, and personality through outstanding photography. Just as the consistent use of the logo builds the brand, so do high quality images that express core experiences. The brand communications should be led by "hero" images that capture the Destination Promise™ and the core experiences.

## Questions

Important questions to be answered during Step Four are:

- Is the name of the place attractive, easy to remember, and appropriate for marketing purposes? How many other places have the same or similar name?

- Have you identified key words, phrases and stories to express the brand?

- Do the logo and tagline capture the spirit of the Destination Promise™?

- Do the city symbols, logo, and taglines have maximum legal protection?

- Do your color pallet, fonts, and designs create a distinctive brand identity?

- Do your photo images support the Destination Promise™ and core experiences?

## CHAPTER TEN

# Step Five: Activation – How Will the Brand Come to Life?

It's now time to orchestrate the communications and on-brand actions that will elicit the desired responses from customers. The long-term success of the brand depends on your correct, consistent, and creative use of all brand components.

There are many publications on the subjects of advertising, public relations, Internet marketing, and brochure production so I will not go into any depth about them here. The focus in this chapter is not to replicate their excellent work, but to outline how to activate and embed the brand identity into these applications.

Producing clear brand guidelines and creative briefs are the best ways to ensure that your brand identity is accurately represented at all times and that all advertising, Web design, signs, brochures, and public relations programs are in tune with the brand strategy. It is particularly important when you have many partners and vendors communicating the brand.

To check that all brand communications are customer-focused and convey enticing benefits, imagine that the customer is looking over your shoulder as you prepare the materials. When you proofread the copy, select an image, or complete the production, imagine that the customer asks you, *"So, what's in it for me?"* This technique helps to maintain a customer-centered approach.

It takes great experiences to sustain great brands. Marketing communications should be lead by core experiences and benefits, and not be littered with facts, member lists and information included only to please internal stakeholders. Marketing applications should portray how the place will make customers feel and must answer their perennial question, *"What's in it for me?"*

Remember, the most powerful, meaningful and appropriate benefits – the emotional rewards – should always be at the forefront. Avoid talking about the city as a series of locations, attractions, and things to see and do. Instead, bring it to life as an experience and make customers feel as though they are already there sensing and feeling it when they read, see, or hear your communications. Make it easy for people to see themselves in the picture. This will make their decision to experience your community for themselves much easier. And don't try to balance the images for political harmony. The customer doesn't care! Additionally, just as you would invest in the best graphic designer you can afford, invest in the best copywriter you can afford as well.

## Integrated Marketing Communications

Integrating your marketing messages is the most effective way to generate the most impactful communications. In a nutshell, this involves carefully synchronizing all advertising, public relations, Web marketing, collateral, direct mail, and other communications. By orchestrating your marketing in this way, you will generate synergy across all applications by exposing customers to multiple, frequent, and consistent brand images and messages, maximizing the return on investment. While you may think that integrated marketing is the domain of destinations with large budgets, it is equally incumbent upon those with small budgets to synchronize their efforts to maximize their impact and effectiveness.

Integrated marketing communications can be even more effective when key partners and messengers in the community become part of the coordinated effort. Some of the applications that can be activated to simultaneously communicate brand messages in an integrated marketing campaign are:

- Advertising
- Billboards
- Broadcast advertising
- Collateral materials
- Décor
- Direct mail
- Display materials
- Email marketing
- Information kiosks
- Online marketing
- Phone system
- Pod casting
- Print advertising
- Promotional events
- Promotional items and souvenirs
- Public relations
- Publications
- Radio advertising
- Sales calls
- Sales manuals
- Signage and wayfinding
- Trade show displays
- Training and education programs
- Uniforms
- Vehicles
- Video / DVD presentations
- Visitor information centers
- Web marketing

So much of the leisure travel advertising by small cities is wasted because little of it adds to the knowledge and meaning that prospective customers have of the place. This is not to say that advertising is useless, it's that their small advertising budgets, their limited reach and frequency, and the use of inappropriate and constantly changing messages render their messages largely ineffective.

Many destinations feel that if they can only produce really great advertising and have a mountain of money to buy media, they will be able to build a great brand. Unfortunately, you can't muscle your way into the modern consumer's mind like that. Brute force marketing that attempts to interrupt customers during their leisure activities such as television watching, driving or reading is nowhere near as effective or efficient as it used to be. Those with the biggest advertising budgets and the most creative advertising don't necessarily win.

Today's customers place low trust in advertising, and that includes travel and tourism advertising as well. These are empowered consumers who are likely to be savvy and discerning. Prospective customers have access to Websites such as tripadvisor.com where they can review the postings of past visitors to destinations, attractors and lodging to verify that a destination or hotel is really suitable for them.

> **Those destinations with the biggest advertising budgets and the most creative advertising don't necessarily win.**

The decision to visit a place usually involves the customer investing a considerable amount of time and perhaps money in researching their options. Customers will base their selections on complex perceptions and attitudes which may have accumulated from a wide variety of sources, and over many years. The challenge for place marketers is to effectively embed their messages into as many concurrent marketing applications as possible.

## Advertising

Advertising, whether it is print, broadcast or online, should always capture and dramatize the essence of the Destination Promise™. It should also consistently leverage the brand personality and benefits to ensure that they are strongly associated with the city.

Wherever possible, advertising should observe the following branding rules of thumb:

- The community's name, logo and tagline are prominently displayed.

- The copy, images and style are true to the Destination Promise™.

- The advertising is consistent with the city's personality and values.

- Don't try to tell the whole story – leave that up to the Website, brochure or other elements of the campaign. Keep copy concise.

- Encourage the prospect to take the next step toward booking or register to receive future updates and information.

While managing the extensive direct mail programs for Australia, I came to the realization that 98% of our initial communications were ignored. Unfortunately, when I review the advertising performance of many small cities, I see that they have yet to come to the same realization. Even fewer have the database marketing systems to address this situation and initiate ongoing communications with their best prospects.

Amazingly enough, some DMOs, after spending anywhere from $20 to $200 per advertising respondent, throw the name and address of the potential visitor in the trash bin after sending the brochure. They have no plan to establish a relationship with the respondent by forming an ongoing dialog to convert them from an inquirer into a satisfied customer. We know that while an inquirer may be considering a particular destination, it may take years before they actually decide to visit the place.

Conrad Levinson, author of *Guerilla Marketing*, estimates it takes nine impressions on a potential customer to get them to take any action, and this does not necessarily include making a booking or doing business with the community. Since only one of every three attempts, on average, gets through to the prospect, that's 27 messages that need to be directed toward the prospect. My personal feeling is that Mr. Levinson's estimate may be on the low side when it comes to destination marketing.

It is not uncommon for the organization to then spend next year's advertising budget trying to find that same person again! Sadly, these are frequently small cities that cannot afford to waste any portion of their marketing budget. A much better option is to develop a database of respondents and categorize their areas of interest. Then, from time to time, they can send the prospect information relevant to their interests, e.g. events, getaways, adventure, etc. Ideally, this can be addressed economically by using email, online newsletters and online PDF brochures.

## Web-based Marketing

The destination's Website should be the central hub for all marketing and communications programs as shown in Figure 5. It should provide the focal point for consumers, media, and travel trade to easily access information, advertising responses, enquiries, and interactive experiences. It has become an important and cost effective vehicle for expressing the brand. However, in order to achieve this, the Website, like other marketing applications must adhere to the brand usage guidelines. The following are some brand-building rules of thumb that should be applied:

**Figure 5: A Web-based Integrated Marketing Campaign**

- The Website is customer-focused, projecting both tangible and emotional benefits.

- The design and content conform to the brand guidelines.

- Engaging and believable images provide the "What's in it for me" answer.

- Database marketing principles are being applied by building profiles of site visitors, inquiries, and advertising respondents according to their areas of interests.

- A seasonal e-newsletter that is strongly identified with the brand identity is distributed to those who have provided permission to communicate with them.

## Public Relations

Why is it that some places seem to be featured more in the media than others? It's not by accident. More than likely you'll find that the city is very media-savvy. Public relations play a valuable role in brand development and enhancing the reputation of the place. Marketing gurus Laura and Al Ries argue in *The Fall of Advertising and The Rise of PR* [32] that public relations is now proving more effective in building a brand than advertising.

Every city should maintain a public relations program irrespective of the size of its budget and resources. This is an essential activity for any place wanting to enhance its attractiveness and reputation, and protect its good name. The most common elements in the community marketer's PR toolkit are media releases, press kits, media visits, media conferences and briefings, promotions, pitches, speeches and sponsorship.

Public relations is highly cost effective for community marketing efforts and can serve to offset the rising cost of advertising. When executed well, a strong PR initiative generates increased visibility, awareness, and interest at a fraction of the cost of paid advertising.

Whenever they appear in magazines, newspapers, online, radio or television, destination articles and features have an enormous ability to motivate and inform. The benefits extend beyond tourism and can frequently project the city as an attractive place to do business and to live. Consumers are more likely to be engaged by, and indeed trust, a first-hand account by a trusted source than from paid advertising. A trade-off for brand marketers is that they will have little if any control over the content and tone of what the media actually chooses to report.

> **Consumers are more likely to be engaged by, and indeed trust, a first-hand account by a trusted source than from paid advertising.**

The following is a checklist to assist in embedding brand messages in public relations programs:

- All communications should reflect the tone and personality of the brand.

- The press kit and media stationery feature the brand's visual identity and provide links to more detailed online information and images.

- Develop three to five key messages that convey the essence of the brand in "sound bites" for speeches and presentations, and several key phrases to be used in written communications.

- Incorporate at least one key attribute and highlight one emotional benefit in all written and spoken communications.

- Train destination spokespeople (at least the CEO, PR staff and sales staff) to integrate those key messages into communications with the media and key clients.

- Track the coverage of key messages in articles, speeches, TV and radio interviews. If they're not being picked-up by the media, analyze why and revise their use accordingly.

- Keep in mind that this is not a one-time endeavor. Repetition is essential for the content of messages to build awareness and preference.

## Brochures and Publications

Despite the advances in online communications and the Internet, brochures continue to play an important role in marketing and visitor satisfaction. However, extreme care should be taken to ensure that they are well designed, thoughtfully written, and carefully distributed. I have seen marketers waste far too much of their budget on brochures and their distribution.

We tend to be led by our emotions and then verify with our logic. The same applies when we make our travel decisions and purchases. Many cities try to promote themselves by using uninteresting lists of local attractions, businesses and services. While this information does have a role later in the decision-making of customers, it is rarely important at an early stage when visitors are developing their initial awareness and image of a destination. Lists of "what to see & do," "where to eat," and "where to stay" alone do not achieve this. Prospective visitors first need to be convinced of what is appealing, special and memorable about the place. To maintain maximum alignment with the brand, brochures should:

- Reflect the Destination Promise™ of the place on the cover.

- Prominently feature the core experiences and their benefits.

- Carefully follow the brand guidelines in regard to typography, logo use, color pallet, and design standards.

- Include copy that is based on the key words, benefits, phrases, and brand stories.

- Clearly demonstrate and answer the *"What's in it for me?"* question.

## Word-of-Mouth

Your customers have never had more power. They have connectivity through all kinds of electronic devices from cell phones, email, Websites, blogs, MySpace and YouTube to instantly reach friends and family around the world – and while they are visiting your city!

Friends and relatives, past visits, customer comments on Web-sites, and the independent advice of guidebooks are highly influential in approximately 80% of travel decisions. I refer to these influences as experience-based or loyalty-based decisions because they have been heavily influenced by the loyalty and past experiences of customers.

On the other hand, advertising, public relations, destination Websites, and publications may have provided the stimulus for only 10-15% of visitors. The customer's decisions based on these mar-keting applications could be regarded as "leap of faith" decisions because they call on the prospective visitor to make a leap of faith in their decision-making and trust what they are reading and seeing in marketing communications.

**.... it's still word-of-mouth that is the most powerful, and technology is amplifying the impact of this highly influential form of communication.**

Despite all of the marketing oppor-tunities today, it's still word-of-mouth that is the most powerful, and technol-ogy is amplifying the impact of this highly influential form of communica-tion. Travel Websites specializing in peer reviews, such as IgoUgo, Trip Advisor, and Lonely Planet's Blue List are favorites among seasoned and nov-ice travelers who use the comments of past visitors to influence their travel decisions. Even individual destinations are now incorporating similar online features such as Travel Oregon's GoSeeOregon.com which allows travelers to share information, tips and recommenda-tions about places to go and things to do in Oregon. This consumer generated internet content underscores the point that your brand is not what you say you are, but what your customers say you are. The challenge for destination marketers in this environment is to influence on-brand communication at critical points of contact with visitors and to constantly monitor this content.

Quite clearly, it is important that city marketers address both the experience-based as well as the leap of faith-based influences in order to grow their markets. My point is that in too many cases the focus is predominantly on the leap of faith-based generators with little or no attention being paid to producing word-of-mouth advocates through outstanding visitor experiences. This does not mean that I regard advertising and other paid leap of faith marketing activities as being of little or no value in building a brand. What I am suggesting is a more holistic view of destination marketing that takes into account the total destination experience. Communities are often too quick to search for new prospects before they have capitalized on the opportunities that might be right in front of them – the low hanging fruit that is easiest to harvest. It is possible, even likely, that your most accessible advocates for positive word-of-mouth are current and past customers, employees, and residents.

An excellent example of the power of staff in influencing future visitation comes from the Main Street associations in Virginia. Time and again, their surveys have shown that the most effective way to promote the monthly events in each community was not through advertising, but by encouraging front line staff to personally invite customers to return for events. For instance, when chatting to customers, they simply ask, "Are you coming along to First Thursday this week?" This simple, friendly opening creates the opportunity to promote an event and extend a personal invitation to come back again. Similar success in positively influencing customer behavior can be seen in the actions of enthusiastic staff in information centers, attractions, lodging, and restaurants around the country. This is also a reminder of the potential power that your front line staff have in projecting your brand, correctly and incorrectly.

## Brand Experiences

I particularly like the way in which Disney's former CEO Michael Eisner referred to the Disney brand when he said, "Our brand is a living entity – and it is enriched or undermined cumulatively

> **"Our brand is a living entity – and it is enriched or undermined cumulatively over time, the product of thousands of small gestures."**
>
> **Michael Eisner**
> **Former CEO, Disney**

over time, the product of thousands of small gestures." Delivering outstanding brand experiences through these gestures across a destination calls for different types of partnerships and involvement in order to involve the most appropriate and influential people.

Tourism Australia's General Manager UK / Europe Rodney Harrex highlighted the priority that Australia places on experiential branding when he said, "The success of Brand Australia is not conveyed by our advertising alone, but through all encounters and experiences with Australia and its people. To achieve this we are transforming the brand from being presented as a trip, vacation or destination to becoming a wholly immersive, aspirational and engaging experience."

Similarly, Nova Scotia, Canada is building its tourism brand around being a destination of experiences that are closely aligned to customer's interests and in which the province has a competitive advantage. Nova Scotia Tourism's executive director Lloyd Banfield says, "In order to really differentiate ourselves in the consumer's mind, we have to focus on what we truly own as a destination of experiences, and be true to them in our communication and product delivery. It is through the development and enhancement of these competitive, unique experiences that we speak to today's customer. This makes music, cuisine and wine, coastal experiences and living history strategic priorities for us."

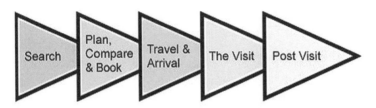

**Figure 6: The Visitor Experience Model**

Destinations that embrace experience delivery to the same extent as Nova Scotia are focused on enhancing their encounters with customers at every point of contact. This can be addressed through experience mapping. Experience mapping is a concept that enables us to consider how customers encounter a place by tracing the five stages in their total destination experience. The model in Figure 6 shows that the experience commences before customers make their reservations or arrive in the city. They are interacting with the place long before they are on the "radar" of city marketers.

This model is useful for analyzing customer's decision-making and satisfaction with key moments in their relationship with the destination. It reflects the fact that as customers proceed from one stage to the next, their behavior, wants and needs change. The five stages of the total destination experience are:

1) *Search:* Here you will find the early Promise Points that influence whether the person becomes a customer for the destination or not. Commonly, these Promise Points include advertising, articles in newspapers, magazines or online, brochures, Websites, guidebooks, word of mouth, emails and past experiences.

2) *Plan, Compare and Book:* Bridging the gap between a potential visitor's consideration of your community and becoming a customer is possibly the greatest challenge facing all destinations. The Promise Points here commonly include fulfilling the questions from prospects and the ease of making transactions and bookings. They may relate to Websites, reservations services, price, conditions and rules, discounts, packages, and staff.

3) *Travel and Arrival:* At this point the experience is well underway, and the journey is an integral part of the total destination experience. The cost, quality, and ease of access and transport can influence attitudes toward the place. Upon arrival in the city, is it easy to find your way around? What are the first impressions? Is there a sense of welcome?

4) *The Visit:* This is the phase where we are most conscious of the experiences associated with a destination. What is the quality of the attractions and their experiences? How are customers interacting with the place? What are the quality and service standards? What is the appropriateness of attractors, signage, brochures, tour guides, taxi drivers, and visitor services?

5) *Post Visit:* This phase is frequently overlooked and does not receive the attention that it deserves to build positive word of mouth and positive memories. What is their reaction to leaving the place, souvenirs and local products, direct mail, and "thank you" letters?

Critical Promise Points may include:

- Access to / within the city
- Advertising
- Appearance / streetscapes
- Architecture
- Attractions
- City gateways
- Cleanliness and safety
- Developers and Investors
- Employees / management
- Events and festivals
- Geographic setting
- Government
- Information access and content
- Landlords
- Lighting and poles
- Maintenance of buildings / public spaces
- Media
- Parking
- Publications
- Public Art
- Reservation systems
- Residents
- Retailers
- Sidewalks and street crossings
- Signs and wayfinding
- Tourism infrastructure
- Visitor services
- Websites

## Experience Management in Action

It helps to consider destinations as experiential products. Their stories, ambience and experiences are inseparable from the place. The following are examples of how some destinations are bringing their brands to life and creatively addressing the challenges of delivering on their promise.

Walking into the visitor information center in Jackson WY you immediately get a sense of the region's personality and essence through interactive displays, natural history exhibits, many sources of information, and an observation deck from where you can see elk grazing in the shadows of the Grand Tetons.

Visitors to Anaheim CA can now sense the Disney experience long before they arrive at the gates of the Magic Kingdom. Disneyland Resort, the district that surrounds Disneyland theme park is fastidious about easy access, readily accessible free transportation, clear wayfinding and signage, and its strong sense of arrival and welcome. Bronze maps of the district have been inlaid into the sidewalk at many intersections surrounding the park to assist pedestrians in easily finding their way around.

The California Gold Rush heritage and the cosmopolitan experiences of Sacramento CA influenced the city's brand strategy and is captured in the tagline *Sacramento. Discover Gold.* This theme inspired the introduction of the *Sacramento Gold Card* which utilizes smart card technology to provide guests with discounted entry to many attractions and restaurants.

Strict design codes for building, landscaping, and streetscapes are employed by Carmel CA, Cannon Beach OR, and Peggy's Cove, Nova Scotia to ensure that the communities retain their individuality and reputations as idyllic seaside communities.

The city of Alhambra CA was originally named after the luxurious palace in the book *The Alhambra* by Washington Irving. This inspired the use of mosaics as a central element of the city's brand identity. The brilliant, bold colors of mosaics are now found connecting the downtown of Alhambra in paving, banners, billboards, store signs and numbering, and wayfinding. In the Canadian province of Alberta, Downtown Red Deer has also used the vibrancy of its brand colors in the street light standards, trash receptacles, tiles on sidewalks and even in the sprucing up of vacant buildings.

Huntington Beach CA is constantly working to sustain its reputation as "Surf City USA™. The city has a distinct flavor based on its authentic surfing culture, which has been part of the fabric of the city for half a century, and is now the epicenter for a new generation of surf enthusiasts. In addition to hosting the biggest surfing event in the world, visitors are immersed in the surfing culture through the International Surfing Museum, the Surf Walk of Fame, and the Surfing Hall of Fame. As if this isn't enough, the city allowed the surfwear retailer, Hollister to install Web cams on the Huntington Pier to transmit live images of the shoreline into its classic cabana-like shops at fifty of its high profile stores nationwide.

Victoria, BC in Canada is known worldwide as *The World's Garden City*. To support this proposition, the City of Victoria has been placing flower baskets in the downtown area since 1937. They now place approximately 1,200 baskets, not including the many baskets displayed by individual businesses. The City's commitment to the "garden city" brand identity is demonstrated by their US $4.5 million annual beautification budget.[33]

Oregon's Washington County has adopted a highly collaborative approach toward experience development integrating the actions of the entities responsible for key niche products. Brian Harney, Director of Marketing for the Washington County Visitors Association said, "To ensure that we can consistently deliver the high quality wine, sport and nature tourism experiences that are promised by our brand, we have established product development partnerships. These groups are designed to be self-sustaining networks so that product providers, many of whom are non-profit entities, can collaborate in enhancing their products and marketing through the unifying themes of our core brand experiences. This is far more advantageous than for each entity to try to go it alone in their product development initiatives and marketing."

## The Brand Manual and Guidelines

Whether it is called the brand manual, handbook, blueprint, toolkit, strategy or guidelines, doesn't really matter. The brand manual provides the guidelines outlining how to accurately project the brand identity and how to deliver the destination's distinctive and compelling experiences. Importantly, it is more than simply the usage guidelines for the logo. It documents the rationale behind the brand, defines how the brand should be adopted and used, and how it should be managed and evaluated over time. These days, a brand manual is just as likely to be available online as it is in a printed form. Baltimore (www.areyouinit.com), Durham (www.durhambrand. com), and Anchorage (www.bigwildlife.net/brand.html) have each launched online brand centers that provide brand partners ready access to the latest information relating to their brand.

## Questions

Important questions to be answered during Step Five are:

- Do your communications successfully answer the customer's perennial question, *"What's in it for me?"*.

- In each brand application or communication, has the Destination Promise' been correctly and creatively expressed?

- How well can you deliver the brand at all Promise Points?

- Are the principles of integrated marketing being used?

- Are details of the brand strategy documented and readily available for partners and stakeholders?

## CHAPTER ELEVEN

# Step Six: Adoption – How Do We Maximize the Support of Stakeholders?

Walt Disney said, "You can dream and create the most wonderful place in the world, but it takes passionate people to make the dream a reality." That may explain why Disney doesn't have staff, it has more than 100,000 cast members who create the Disney Magic. Walt recognized that if Mickey, Frontierland, Main Street, and the Pirates of the Caribbean were going to delight millions of guests it would take dedicated, skilled, trained, and enthusiastic partners to create the *"Happiest Place on Earth."*

While there are many tools in a destination marketer's arsenal, as there are for Disney, it is people who are ultimately the most influential and credible communicators of brand experiences. Behind the scenes, it takes people to drive the strategies, decisions, designs, creativity, management, systems, and policies that influence communications and the customer experiences. They may be marketers, engineers, business and civic leaders, educators, and service professionals. In the case of a community it also involves political leaders, retailers, entrepreneurs, investors, and front line staff to develop a compelling and sustainable brand.

As the Disney experience shows, only people can fulfill a brand promise and be responsible for the brand's ongoing vitality. They must be true to the Destination Promise( and breathe life into the many Promise Points that add value and create those memorable and satisfying experiences for customers.

Pocono Mountains Visitors Bureau Executive Director Robert Uguccioni espouses this same philosophy. "An adoption or enculturation process will require a long-term commitment, influencing a culture and building a brand cannot happen overnight. In the first stage, we have created an e-learning program that will be provided free of charge to our members and the community at large to promote our new brand message and create a sense of inclusion and the understanding that the delivery of the brand promise is in each individual's hands."

## Buy-in Should Have Started Months Ago!

We know of countries, cities and regions that have launched a new brand with great fanfare, only to see it fall flat. Key stakeholders and partners didn't support it because the brand was developed behind closed doors with little or no consultation with anyone outside of the DMO. Instead, the DMO should have been working to avoid this situation by building buy-in and support from the start of the project.

This early buy-in will help to orchestrate a 'soft landing' for the brand and it will be well received, endorsed, and supported by key public, non-profit, and private sector organizations, stakeholders and trade partners.

## Who Should be Involved?

A destination brand is as strong as its weakest advocate. The successful implementation of the brand strategy will require actions by more than just the Chamber of Commerce or CVB. It will require the long-term advocacy, passion, and support by dozens, and maybe hundreds, of local individuals and organizations.

Just as during the Middle Ages when the entire village contributed to building the city's cathedral, today it takes the whole "village" to build and sustain the city brand. During the Middle Ages it took generations of masons, laborers, glassmakers, carpenters and so on to do their job over hundreds of years. In building a city brand, just about everybody has a role to play because they can strengthen or weaken it whenever they, or their work, comes in contact with the city's customers.[34]

I have come to realize that the Adoption stage of brand planning can be very much about change management and destinations may have to embrace many of those principles. Brand management may call for changes in behavior and relationships for the DMO, its Board, and partners for the brand to be built from the inside out. It may call for variations to structures, systems, recruitment, processes, attitudes, and "the way we do things around here." Preparing to deliver and manage a strong brand may directly impact on everything that the organization does.

> **Brand management may call for changes in behavior and relationships for the DMO, its Board, and partners for the brand to be built from the inside out.**

There are possibly hundreds of prospective brand partners, stakeholders, and interested parties across the city. Consistent and repeated education and information is essential to maintain their focus, both as a refresher and because there is frequent staff turnover in so many positions that affect the brand communications and delivery.

There are many agencies, organizations, individuals, and teams in the community that are responsible for communicating the brand in one way or another in both official and unofficial capacities. For some, such as local government, DMO, Chamber of Commerce, and the tourism industry, it should be central to their destination or place marketing mission. There are others such as media, developers, real estate agents, and service staff who project a positive, and sometimes inadvertently a negative or dated, image of the city who need to understand your mission.

Most city governments don't think in terms of marketing, but they are often attuned to the related concept of enhancing and protecting the city's good name and encouraging business growth.

Some individuals such as politicians, sports stars, entertainers, business leaders, academics and celebrities frequently find themselves in the role of official and unofficial ambassadors for a city, whether they set out to be or not. Then there are the hotels, attractions, tour operators, and others who are actively trying to entice visitors to the city. And we can't forget about the universities and colleges, retailers, developers, and employers. Each of them may be telling outsiders to visit, invest, relocate or study in the area.

Many communities make the mistake of not sufficiently informing and engaging external stakeholders and partners during the launch. This group, comprising meeting planners, relocation specialists, media, travel trade, and group travel operators, should be informed of the brand strategy and how they can support and use the brand as soon as possible. True success will only happen if key partners and stakeholders are motivated, totally understand the brand, know how to use it, and genuinely want to support it.

Don't worry – you don't have to go as far as Chinese authorities in encouraging on-brand behavior! According to China Daily, the country now has an official etiquette watchdog and, keen to ensure nothing mars the Beijing image during the 2008 Olympic Games, has launched several campaigns to curb "uncivilized" behavior "such as spitting and littering." Among the initiatives, the 11th of every month is now "voluntary wait in line" day designed to eliminate pushing and shoving in favor of orderly lines.[35]

## The Adoption Strategy

The number one objective at this point is to encourage understanding, adoption and correct use – one brand, many partners, one voice. The adoption strategy should outline the goals, techniques, and messages that will boost support and use of the brand by stakeholders, residents, partners and other messengers. It calls for you to identify the individuals and organizations most important to the health of the brand and allow them to initiate the actions needed to adopt and support the brand.

The leading adoption goals are to encourage people to:

- Understand the brand strategy including the Destination Promise™ and brand identity elements
- Understand how they can support and correctly use the brand
- Consider how they can help make the on-brand behavior easier for others
- Know how it affects their role and everyday responsibilities
- Deliver outstanding brand experiences

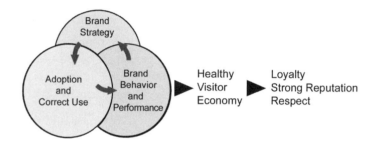

**Figure 7: The Brand Loyalty Process**

The adoption goals bring into focus the difference between a brand and a tagline. These goals cannot be achieved if the brand strategy is simply a tagline or logo.

Figure 7 demonstrates the benefits that can come from broad stakeholder adoption and how their correct brand behavior leads to loyalty, respect and a destination with a strong reputation and healthy visitor economy.

## Ready to Launch!

There are no definitive rules for how to roll out the public launch of a destination brand strategy. Some prefer to keep everything under wraps until a wide range of marketing applications can be revealed at the same time with great fanfare, while others choose to have a "soft" launch by revealing the main elements of the brand and an explanation of how it was developed, and then releasing various elements over the following months. Whichever path you choose, you should have prototypes to demonstrate how various applications are likely to look.

During the launch you can communicate why you adopted a branded approach, how it was developed, future plans, and how everyone can be involved and contribute toward its success. It is particularly important that staff, partners and stakeholders understand the rationale behind the brand and the level of community consultation that has taken place. Support for a community-based brand is always enhanced when constituents know that the process was inclusive and not created behind closed doors by "the usual suspects." Be sure to acknowledge the efforts of individuals who aided in the development phases and particularly give credit to those who made extraordinary contributions. No doubt your Brand Advisory Group deserves special kudos.

**It is particularly important that staff, partners and stakeholders understand the rationale behind the brand and the level of community consultation that has taken place.**

After Durham's brand strategy was completed, Reyn Bowman, the CVB's President and Shelly Green, the Chief Operating Officer conducted sixty face-to-face meetings with government, community, business, and education leaders across the community. This enabled them to not only generate a clear understanding of the brand, but to also stimulate wide community acceptance and use of the brand by groups as diverse as Duke University, the Research Triangle Park, the Durham Bulls Baseball team and neighborhood groups.

President of Yakama Valley WA Visitors & Convention Bureau, John Cooper advises, "Plan to carefully orchestrate the launch with a detailed plan that includes media and community relations, the event launch format, and stakeholder briefings. You can't expect the brand to gain traction in the community without a concerted effort. Give consideration to who should speak at the launch and who are the best spokespersons to publicly lend their support to the effort. We found it very valuable to meet with the editorial boards of newspapers and to treat all media equally in distributing information about the brand." Cooper added, "No matter how much research, consultation and agreement there may have been in the creative process be prepared for the criticisms and possible misunderstandings. It pays to do your homework and prepare for the inevitable barbs with responses (which in some cases may be no response at all). Be sure that prime stakeholders are informed and are also ready to respond to possible criticisms with the suggested talking points. Encourage them to hold tight and ride out possible storms."

In stark contrast to many other destinations, the Canadian Tourism Commission launched its new brand in stages stretching over more than a year and a half. The Brand Canada team began by launching the idea and rationale of the brand, followed by the tagline (*Canada. Keep Exploring.*) some six months later, and didn't announce a final logo and visual identity for almost another year. As a result, the brand was well understood and already widely adopted and endorsed by the industry by the time the logo launched. By not offering up a sacrificial logo and tagline, the CTC forced people to listen and think, and not just react.[36]

There are many approaches that you can take to inform stakeholders about the brand and demonstrate how they can support the program. They include:

- An online brand center
- Billboards
- Direct mail
- Email communications

- Media releases and interviews
- Newsletters
- One-on-one briefings
- Presentations and seminars

Among the ways that the Seattle CVB chose to unveil its new Seattle destination brand was to hang a huge 360-degree mural that read *metronatural*™ from the top of the city's most visible landmark, the Space Needle. Banners were strategically placed around the city and a high profile kick-off party for stakeholders added even more visibility and buzz.

Grants Pass OR quickly introduced its brand identity to residents in a similar way, by designing new street banners and directional signs for use throughout the city. Norfolk VA, because of its seaport location, adopted a mermaid as its symbol and she was soon seen throughout the city on everything from statues, stained glass, and promotional items to Websites and brochures.

## Questions

Important questions to be answered during Step Six are:

- Who should be involved? What do they need to know? What do you want them to do?

- Have appropriate briefing and training programs been designed and implemented?

- Have you developed plans for the launch?

- Have you considered the policies, regulations and roles that will impact on-brand behavior?

## CHAPTER TWELVE

# Step Seven: Action and Afterward – How Do We Keep the Brand Fresh and Relevant?

Your job isn't over after the brand's launch – in fact, it's just beginning! Branding is long-term and cumulative. It is an ongoing organizing and management principle that needs continued focus to shape and deliver the brand over time. You can never afford to get comfortable or complacent because it involves a constant battle to remain relevant and attractive. It doesn't take long for what may have been a thriving destination to lose favor or momentum and fall victim to trends that it did not pay attention to.

The sooner key stakeholders embrace the brand, the sooner cohesive brand experiences will thrive. The brand's long-term vitality depends on how well the DMO or lead agency manages five issues. They are:

1. Brand Leadership
2. Brand Management
3. Brand Communications
4. Experience Management
5. Monitoring and Evaluation

## 1. Brand Leadership

Successful brands are lead from the top and owned at the grassroots and by customers. The high level influence is termed brand leadership and provides the strategic focus and prioritization for long-term results, partnerships, and fosters the competitive advantage that will distinguish the community.

Some of the brand leadership actions that should be considered are:

*Strategic Planning:* The brand strategy must be integrated into the planning processes of the Chamber, CVB and local government. As appropriate, it should be reflected in their strategies. The brand should not be considered as simply an "add-on." It has to be an integral element of every action that has an impact on the organization's customers to ensure that it fulfills the Destination Promise™.

*Cross-City Partnerships:* Delivering the Destination Promise™ cannot be the sole province of the DMO or Chamber of Commerce – it requires a shared responsibility. The branding objectives must engage leaders, organizations and individuals who can orchestrate the on-brand behavior, regulations, policies, investments, and plans. Ideally, it should include city planners, architects, transport specialists, landlords, and developers, as well as elected, non-profits, government and business leaders.

*Brand Champions:* Great brands need people who will champion their cause. They are internal and external catalysts for the vision, values, and development of the brand.

*Change Management:* A brand strategy frequently presents opportunities that require the DMO and its partners to adapt to new circumstances to attain their true potential. Effectively managing the new brand requires that there be no walls or "silos" in which people and organizations isolate their on-brand actions. Leaders should embrace changes, alleviate fear and constantly evaluate how to create a better playing field for the brand to be a winner. Ultimately, success goes to those that pay attention to the politics, systems, processes, people, resources, and priorities that underpin their promises. It is not simply the hourly employees at the customer interface, or the executives and strategic priorities behind them who are responsible for this – it's everyone!

## Brand Champions on the Rogue

The Grants Pass OR brand identity is centered on the Rogue River that runs through downtown and has inspired whitewater enthusiasts, writers such as Zane Grey, filmmakers, and hundreds of weekend artists for around 100 years. It has also inspired a civic-minded local bank president, Brady Adams, to help reconnect the downtown with its celebrated river and establish Grants Pass as one of the best river cities in America. To make this connection and to realize the vision, Brady and his Evergreen National Bank have stepped in as true brand champions. In 2005, the bank even developed a master plan as a tool for interested parties to use when considering changes in the city.

They are employing distinctive northwest-style fishing lodge architectural designs, public art, events and urban design to reconnect the river area to the community. Over the next ten years, the bank will work to re-vitalize the riverfront and make it more accessible to locals and visitors alike. In this way Grants Pass will build a stronger community, deliver on its brand promise and realize its vision.

The plan involves reclaiming the riverfront, introducing more appropriately designed buildings, a larger than life *Wildlife Bronze Park*, events inspired by public art such as *Bearfest*, and an iconic 1930s era touring bus to provide free transport around downtown. I particularly like the "River Kids" comprising a dozen or more life-sized bronze statues along 5th and 6th streets of children engaged in a variety of adventures on the river set in the 1930s, 40s and 50s. What makes the statues even more engaging is that they are based on real people who lived in the city during those periods.

The Grants Pass *River District Project* is an excellent example of private-public collaboration bringing a destination brand to life and will firmly reposition the city with key audiences. It is an even stronger example of a true brand champion from outside of the traditional tourism industry. Brady is truly an innovative and visionary man. He says, "I am not in the banking industry. I am in the tourism industry. In order for the bank to be successful … the community has to be successful. A healthy community can build a tourism industry that attracts affluent retirees who then consider settling in Grants Pass."

## 2. Brand Management

Brand management is tactical and has a short-term focus, compared to the long-term focus of brand leadership. It should not happen by accident or through *ad hoc* efforts. Orchestrating branded behavior takes a concerted effort to monitor and communicate with a wide variety of people, organizations, and interests.

Brands bring with them the challenge of being innovative to ensure that the brand remains fresh and exciting. Brand management is about shaping and managing perceptions and opinions – and that's not easy! Periodically brand managers have to re-energize partners, stakeholders, and even customers.

Brand management embraces more than the traditional marketing functions. It calls for every customer-facing aspect of the city to be aligned with the Destination Promise™. While the traditional view of destination marketing may have been centered around advertising, public relations, sales and publications, today it extends to issues such as gateways, streetscapes, infrastructure, visitor services, partnerships, and experience development.

*The Brand Steward:* This executive should be selected at the start of the process. It is his or her job to keep the brand development phase on track. Brand stewardship involves "inside out" actions focusing on their organization and partners to influence the ways they think and act when projecting the brand to external audiences.

Just as a financial auditor has authority, this person must also be empowered with the authority to do the job. If no-one is specifically designated in this role, brand adoption and use is likely to be patchy and applications may stray from their prescribed path. Without a brand steward, there is the possibility that things may revert back to the "bad old ways." If high level drive and commitment are absent there is the possibility that things may never actually leave the "bad old ways."

The brand steward must maintain a vigilant eye on all uses of the brand identity. While innovation and creativity are essential for a vibrant brand, there should be no tolerance for variations from the brand parameters that are outlined in the manual. Just one small variation after another and suddenly you're way off strategy. Managing the brand involves much more than the technical oversight of how the logo and color palette should be used. It calls for close attention to every critical Promise Point and communication with customers.

*Brand Talent:* Working under the direction of the brand steward should be a team of talented people. Many may be outside vendors and marketing specialists, depending on the size of the organization. Periodically, we see small communities try to design their Website, brochures and advertising by using a local graphic designer or staff member who does not have the skills or experience to creatively and correctly project the brand. This is a situation where buying local can harm the community. Just as you may go to the best medical specialist outside of town, you should also go to the best and most appropriate marketing vendors. Even if it means paying a bit more, the overall benefit to the community by way of extra economic activity will make it worthwhile.

*Continual Brand Education:* This is essential to ensure that key partners and stakeholders continue to be engaged and understand the ways that they can best represent the brand. Santa Monica CA has conducted ongoing brand training for CVB staff, as well as a specially designed training program for the sales personnel of hotels and attractions, meeting planners and the travel trade. Similarly, in Woodburn OR the Chamber of Commerce regularly schedules free training seminars to ensure that front-line lodging and retail staff are providing high quality service and understand how to project the community's brand in a positive manner.

## 3. Brand Communications

When the brand messages are consistently, correctly and creatively communicated to the right target audiences at the right time, they should trigger the desired emotions, appeal to customer logic, and enhance the brand image. Every person conveying brand messages must always ask the question, "Have I correctly and creatively reinforced the Destination Promise' in this decision or activity?" This applies to every opportunity to reflect and reinforce the brand, whether selecting a photographic image, choosing the color of carpet for a trade show booth, or proofing copy for a publication or Website.

## 4. Experience Management

How will you ensure that the Destination Promise™ materializes at every Promise Point? Malcolm Allan, of *placebrands* in London says, "Obviously, not every single action, policy, investment or event of the city will be fully 'on brand' and some of them will even likely be 'off brand'. It is important that the key stakeholders realize and identify which of the multitude of their activities have significant impact on the brand that they wish to realize."[37]

There are two types of experiences that are priorities for destination marketers to manage and monitor. The first are the *core brand experiences*. These are the encounters that are essential to the experiential themes outlined in your brand platform and Destination Promise™. The second are the broader *Promise Points* that play a crucial role throughout the customer's total destination experience.

The core brand experiences are likely to be centered on the main attractors, while Promise Points can potentially involve almost any aspect of the place, including individuals and organizations outside of the city such as tour operators and media.

Promise Points can be found during each stage of the total destination experience and may have a profound impact on the customer's satisfaction level. In the early stages of contact, some of these Promise Points are so critical that failure to satisfy the person could result in them not proceeding with plans, and then may be lost to a competitor. Critical to successful experience management is monitoring customer expectations and satisfaction with key elements of the destination experiences, and close collaboration with partners to meet and exceed those expectations.

## 5. Monitoring and Evaluation

With the brand now launched, it is vital that you closely monitor and manage its progress and make adjustments when necessary. This is not necessarily an expensive or time-consuming exercise. While several performance measures such as visitor numbers, information requests received online, in-person or via phone, lodging tax revenue, occupancy levels, visitor spending, and advertising responses may already be monitored, there are a number of other brand health metrics that should be appraised at least once a year.

Brad Dean of Myrtle Beach Area Chamber of Commerce, gives us valuable advice in saying, "One difficulty we ran into, and still deal with nearly two years later, is defining measurable, planned outcomes. Once everyone agrees with the branding process, there is a sense of camaraderie. Everyone is talking about "the brand" and seemingly buying in. But the mistake we made was to not clearly define our measurements of success. We allowed the defining of the brand to overtake our strategic implementation of the brand, and within a few months the measurable outcomes (in our case, phone calls and Web visitors) had declined. Almost immediately, everyone becomes 'like maybe this branding thing is not all it's cracked up to be'. If I were guiding the process today, I would make certain any real (or perceived) outcomes are monitored and managed accordingly."

Research is a high priority for the brand management of Durham CVB. CEO and President Reyn Bowman explains, "We conduct a variety of public opinion and satisfaction surveys to help us monitor the brand and ensure that it continues to be relevant and respected by both internal and external audiences. Importantly, this helps us keep the customer and the performance of our visitor experiences front and center in our decision-making."

Monitor the following six indicators to ensure that your brand remains relevant and meaningful over time.

1.  Stay focused on the demographics, behavior and satisfaction of your target audiences.

2.  Keep your visual identity and communications fresh and creative.

3.  Ensure that your positioning and Destination Promise™ stay meaningful.

4.  Watch overall trends that can impact customer demand and behavior, such as technological changes.

5.  Monitor Promise Points to ensure that they are aligned with customer needs and reflect the brand.

6.  Observe that core experiences remain meaningful and of high quality.

Some of the criteria and methods that you can use to evaluate the brand beyond the normal visitor performance measures include:

| Performance Indicator | Method |
|---|---|
| *Brand adoption by stakeholders* | Review commercial, government, cultural and community organizations to gauge the extent of their adoption of the brand – beyond the logo and tagline use. Consider the extent and accuracy of their adoption of brand messages, images, and personality. |
| *Community pride and brand support* | Conduct a survey of residents, businesses, tourism, government and other interested organizations. Repeat every two years. |
| *Co-operative support* | Track the level of participation in DMO co-operative marketing. |
| *Customer profiles* | Assess shifts in customer profiles and source markets. |

| | |
|---|---|
| *Customer satisfaction* | Conduct ongoing customer surveys to monitor satisfaction with your experience delivery. |
| *Brand consistency* | Review the appearance and content of all marketing materials that project the city including those produced outside of the area, e.g. tour operators. |
| *Media coverage* | Monitor media coverage for use of the desired brand messages. |
| *Stakeholder feedback* | Survey key stakeholders, partners, and city messengers to explore and monitor brand development issues. |
| *Attitudes toward the city* | Monitor shifts in customer attitudes, perceptions, and image of the city. |

## Questions

Important questions to be answered during Step Seven are:

- Is the brand totally integrated into the plans of city marketers?

- Is an annual brand audit conducted?

- Are the structure, processes, and recruitment policies of the DMO tied to the delivery of the Destination Promise™?

# In Conclusion

The brand planning that you conduct for your city should be one of the most rewarding events in your career. It presents opportunities for learning and moving to new levels of performance, for uniting partners, and for sharpening every aspect of your strategic marketing activities. Most of all, it should contribute toward the increased economic and social well-being of your community, and that will be the greatest reward of all.

I hope that this book clarified the concepts and processes involved in branding destinations and I wish you every success in your destination branding endeavors. Good Luck!

If you would like to share your branding experiences and success stories for future editions or if you have comments about this book, please contact me at billb@DestinationBranding.com.

# APPENDIX

# DESTINATION BRANDING TERMS

The following terms and definitions are provided to assist your understanding of some of the concepts involved in destination branding.

### Brand

A brand is the source of a distinctive promise for customers from a product, service or place. Everything that a marketing organization does in collaboration with its partners and community should be oriented around delivering and constantly enhancing this promise.

### Brand Architecture

This is the family tree or hierarchy of how various associated brand entities are named, organized and relate to each other.

### Brand Associations

These associations (positive and negative) are what customers think of when they hear or see the destination's brand name, tagline, or symbols. In the case of Las Vegas, these may include desert, hot, The Strip, neon signs, gambling, Wayne Newton, etc.

### Brand Awareness

This relates to the degree to which the destination's name is present in the minds of prospective customers. When people are exposed to the name of a destination they should immediately recognize it and form specific positive associations.

### Band Culture

Brand culture aligns the commitment and behavior of stakeholders and partners with the Destination Promise™ and enables the place to deliver its brand experiences. It involves getting all stakeholders "on the same page."

## Brand Equity

The accumulated loyalty, awareness, and financial value of the brand over time.

## Brand Essence

The "heart and soul" or the DNA of the brand and relates to its fundamental nature. It should be short, crisp and rich in meaning, e.g. the brand essence of Las Vegas could be "adult freedom."

## Brand Identity

The brand identity comprises the unique set of visual, auditory, and other stimuli that project the brand through its many applications in order to shape market perceptions. These include the benefits, logo, fonts, tagline, colors, images, and in some cases the special brand smells and sounds.

## Brand Image

The accumulated impressions or perceptions formed by the customers arising from their exposure to the brand. These may be positive, negative, or even neutral. For Las Vegas, this may be "a great place where you are free to do anything you want, whenever you want."

## Brand Loyalty

This is often considered the single most important outcome of a branding strategy. It may be best measured through repeat transactions, referrals, and the nature of the customer's spending patterns. Importantly, brand loyalty also includes the staff, stakeholders, partners, media and others engaged in presenting, delivering and sustaining the brand experience.

## Brand Management

The process of ensuring that the brand's value and promises are maintained and consistently delivered.

## Brand Partners

Those individuals and organizations that are instrumental in the promotion and delivery of the city's promised brand experience.

## Brand Personality

This describes the destination using human personality traits. Las Vegas traits may be fun loving, gregarious, flamboyant and indulgent.

## Brand Platform

The brand platform provides the foundation on which the Destination Promise™ and all future brand experiences will be based. It includes the brand vision, values, benefits and personality.

## Brand Portfolio

In the context of a community or destination, the portfolio refers to the related product categories including tourism, economic development, education, investment, and relocation activities that benefit from the reputation of the brand.

## Brand Positioning

Brand positioning establishes what we want customers to think and feel about the destination. It relates to the position in consumer's minds (and hearts) that we want to occupy.

## Brand Values

The principles that the city and its constituents believe in and live by. They are the guiding principles by which residents want their community to grow and be shared with others.

## Brand Vision

The brand vision clarifies the high-level role that the brand will play in assisting the city achieve its long-term vision and goals.

## Community or City Messengers

These are the individuals and organizations whose communications are influential in shaping the external image of the community. They may include politicians, celebrities, marketers, media, travel organizations and local product.

**Core Experiences**
These are the encounters that are essential to sustaining your positioning and delivering your Destination Promise™.

**Destination Promise™**
The Destination Promise™ encapsulates the positioning, benefits and value proposition that distinguishes the place from competitors. It acts as a vision and roadmap to deliver superior value to customers and forms the driving force for all marketing and experience delivery efforts in order to establish competitive advantage.

**DMO**
A destination marketing organization and may also be referred to as a destination management organization. This term is intended to embrace Convention & Visitors Bureaus, Chambers of Commerce, local government entities, downtown associations, Main Street associations, economic development authorities and other similar organizations that may be responsible for the marketing and management of a destination.

**Overarching Brand**
This is the brand that provides the umbrella embracing all aspects of the city. It may also be called the domain, "all of place" or umbrella brand.

**Promise Points**
These are the most critical and manageable moments or points where the Destination Promise™ can be enhanced or devalued.

**Value Proposition**
The benefits that provide the rationale for customers to select one brand over another.

# END NOTES

1    DMAI ."CVB Organizational & Financial Profile", *Destination Marketing News*, (2005).

     http://www.iacvb.org/E-Newsletter/enews_web.asp?missue_id=241

2    Bill Geist. "You've Been Brandalized", *Zeitgeist Consulting Newsletter* (Summer 2006).

     http://www.zgeist.com/brandelized.html

3    Whisper Brand Strategy Consultants, "How to Choose a Branding Firm", July 8, 2006,

     http://www.whisperbrand.com/blog/2006/07/how-to-choose-a-branding-firm/

4    US Census Bureau, "Statistical Abstract of the United States", December 15, 2006,

     http://www.census.gov/prod/www/statistical-abstract.html

5    Rebecca Gardyn. "Packaging Cities", *American Demographics Magazine*, (January 2002).

6    Janelle Barlow and Paul Stewart. *Branded Customer Service* (San Francisco: Berrett-Koehler, 2004).

7    Nigel Morgan et al. *Destination Branding* (Oxford: Butterworth Heinemann, 2002).

8    Toledo Convention & Visitors Bureau. "doToledo. do what refreshes you", *Toledo Brand Strategy*.

9    Steve Wright, "Waikiki Tourism Brand Set to Re-Launch", *The Tourism Marketing Blog*, 17 April 2007,

     http://cblog.brandcanadablog.com/2007/04/17/waikiki-tourism-brand-set-to-relaunch.aspx

10   Alpen Rose Inn, "Leavenworth Washington History",

     http://www.alpenroseinn.com/Leavenworth_History.html

11  Rebecca Gardyn. "Packaging Cities", *American Demographics Magazine*, (January 2002).

12  Kurt Burkhart. "CVB Eyes Brand Marketing for City", *Carlsbad Chamber of Commerce Business Journal*, June 5, 2005, http://www.carlsbad.org/EditionDetail.aspx?aid=109

13  Duane Knapp and Gary Sherwin, *Destination BrandScience* (DMAI, 2005).

14  Al Ries and Laura Ries, The 22 *Immutable Laws of Branding* (HarperCollins Business, 1999).

15  George Whitfield. "Mountains Don't Smile Back", *DMO World e-Newsletter* No. 2 (Jan. 2005), http://www.frontlinecommunication.co.uk/dmoworld/academy1.html

16  David Taylor, *The Brand Gym* (Chichester UK: John Wiley & Sons Ltd, 2003), 93.

17  Whisper Brand Strategy Consultants, "Theory of Adulation", January 14, 2006, http://www.whisperbrand.com/blog/2006/01/theory-of-adulation/

18  Civic Strategies Inc. "What Comes After Incorporation?", September 23, 2006 http://civicstrategies.com/resources/issues/image.htm+%22what+comes+after+incorporation%3F%22&hl=en&ct=clnk&cd=4&gl=us (April 2, 2007).

19  Sonia Krisnan. "In growing areas, a tale of too-similar cities", *The Seattle Times*, September 19, 2006, http://archives.seattletimes.nwsource.com/cgibin/texis.cgi/web/vortex/display?slug=cityidentity21e&date=20060919&query=tale+of+two+similar+cities

20  Geoff Ayling. *Rapid Response Advertising* (Warriewood NSW: Business & Professional Publishing Pty, 1998), 87.

21  Morgan et.al.

22  G. Warnaby et al. "Marketing UK Towns and Cities as Shopping Destinations", *Journal of Marketing Management*, Vol 18, No. 9/10 (2002), 877-904.

23   Maureen Littlejohn. "The Rebranding of CVB's and Leading The Change", *Convene*, May 2005,

     http://www.pcma.org/resources/convene/archives/displayArticle.
     asp?ARTICLE_ID=5016

24   Hartford – New England's Rising Star. *The Hartford Image Project Partners – Facts at a Glance*, March 2005,

     http://www.hartford.com/press_room/factsaaglance.pdf

25   Historic Richmond Region – Easy to Love
     http://www.richmond.com/easytolove/usebrand.aspx

26   Maureen Littlejohn. "The Rebranding of CVB's and Leading The Change", *Convene*, May 2005,

     http://www.pcma.org/resources/convene/archives/displayArticle.
     asp?ARTICLE_ID=5016

27   Fort Worth Star Telegram November 8, 2005.

28   Houston Chronicle December 1, 2006.

29   Maureen Littlejohn. "The Rebranding of CVB's and Leading The Change", *Convene*, May 2005,

     http://www.pcma.org/resources/convene/archives/displayArticle.
     asp?ARTICLE_ID=5016

30   Doug Traub, *The Branding of Huntington Beach*, Fall 2006,
     http://www.surfcityusa.com/about/HB_Fall2006_coverstory.pdf

31   Steve Wright, "The High Cost of Protecting a Brand", *The Tourism Marketing Blog*,19 April 2007,
     http://cblog.brandcanadablog.com/2007/04/17/the-high-cost-of-
     protecting-a-brand.aspx

32   Al Ries and Laura Ries, *The Fall of Advertising and Rise of PR*, (New York: HarperCollins Publishers, 2002).

33   The City of Victoria, http://www.victoria.ca/common/index.shtml

34   Adapted from Marty Neumeier, *The Brand Gap*, (Indianapolis: New Riders Publishing, 2003), 52.

35  Reuters. "China Cuts Down on Spitting, Litter", *China Daily*, updated 08
    May 2007,
    http://www.chinadaily.com.cn/china/2007-05/08/content_867366.htm

36  Steve Wright, *The Tourism Marketing Blog*,
    http://cblog.brandcanadablog.com/

37  Malcolm Allan, *placebrands*, www.placebrands.net

# ABOUT THE AUTHOR

B ill Baker is founder and President of Total Destination Management and has more than 30 years of destination branding and marketing experience in 25 countries. Bill is recognized internationally as a thought leader and for his pioneer work in creating brand strategies for destinations and communities of all sizes. He works with Convention & Visitors Bureaus, Chambers of Commerce, local government and national tourism offices in the US and abroad.

Bill has developed successful tourism and economic development marketing strategies for dozens of cities and regions throughout the United States. He has been directly involved in some of the most respected and successful destination branding campaigns in the USA, including Australia's highly acclaimed "Shrimp on the Barbie," which he directed for seven years. He also produced tourism strategies for the Sydney 2000 Olympic Games and dozens of communities in Australia, and has provided strategic counsel to destinations around the world including Hong Kong, India, Macau, and Saudi Arabia.

In recognition of his expertise, Bill has been interviewed by CNN, The Travel Channel, New York Times, Los Angeles Times, Forbes, Inc, and many other leading media outlets. He is always in demand as a speaker on destination branding where he energizes seminars and educational forums in the USA and abroad.

After having lived on three continents, Bill now resides in Portland, Oregon with his wife Joan and daughters, Renee and Kate.

If you would like information on Bill's
availability to keynote your conference, visit
www.DestinationBranding.com/speaking.

To contact Bill email
BillB@DestinationBranding.com.

# THE DESTINATION BRANDING
# MASTER WORKSHOP

D o you want to accelerate your branding efforts? Schedule a *Destination Branding Master Workshop* for your Board or marketing committee with Bill Baker, the author of *Destination Branding for Small Cities*.

This energizing and stimulating workshop is custom-designed to fast track destination branding programs and takes you to the next level in destination marketing. A *Destination Branding Master Workshop* lays the groundwork for your brand planning process. It will encourage common understanding of destination branding, what it is, how it works, and its benefits for your community and partners.

In addition to demystifying branding, during the second part of the workshop Bill will lead discussions specific to branding your community. The Workshop features practical exercises to jump start your planning, avoid pitfalls and address the issues that are critical for you to build a strong and meaningful destination brand.

The *Destination Branding Master Workshop* can be custom-designed for sessions ranging from two to six hours.

For more information visit
www.DestinationBranding.com/workshop.